A (Not So) Enlightened Youth

My Uneasy Road to Awareness:
A Guide to Finding Yourself from Within

By: Koi Fresco

A (Not So) Enlightened Youth

Table of Contents

PART 1

PART 2

A (Not So) Enlightened Youth

Prologue

This was never one of my goals in life.

I want you all to understand that. I never grew up thinking I would one day write a book like this or that I would somehow create a transition for the thoughts cluttering my head to instead occupy the ink on the pages of a book. It was just never once part of the plan.

That's the thing about life though, it never really seems to be about the plan in the first place.

I mean we all have one or two. Maybe more. But regardless of the ideal scenarios that play on repeat in our minds, day after day, what happens in-between seems to be the true essence of what defines us. What seemingly defines who we really are.

That's what this book is after all. The words that will come to fruition in this story of my life and awakening are just that.

The in-betweens. The things I never planned. The things I never saw coming.

I have to admit just a few years ago, I could never have envisioned myself writing more than ten or so pages in a row, no matter what the reason may have been.

Yet here I am, sitting on my porch, listening the constant motion of the wind while staring at the screen of a laptop. All with the audacity to assume I can not only write hundreds of pages of content, but that I'll be able to do so successfully, in a way that makes sense not just to me, but to you, the reader.

In a way this might be my own personal version of therapy. We all need our drug, our vice, our escape from the nonstop movement of the world around us. Some of us never find it, and some of us are just now discovering it, the same way I am at this very moment. This experience itself will undoubtedly wind up changing me. Even more so than the events that will transpire.

So as long as you understand that this book is not a work of art, or a rigid belief system being instilled upon you. That what's to come is quite honest a work in progress itself, we should be fine. Because my life so far is not exactly what one would consider artistic or predictable. If so it would probably be quite the average painting at this point in all honesty.

Just because I decided to take these occurrences & guides and place them on paper, gives them no more validity or importance than anyone else's. This life is something we are all forced to experience together. That being said please remember, there is no dictatorship or claim to the perceived importance of one human experience over another's.

Do we create one socially? Sure. Does it exist on a conscious plane? Not at all.

The curveballs that occur in our lives are what inevitably shape it. And it just so happens my experiences shaped me into the person I am today. Young. Full of faults and failures. But one who understands the importance of spreading awareness nonetheless.

I am the totality of my conscious endeavors & experiences. So are you. If at any point while reading these stories and methods for awakening,you feel confused, or behind or simply doubtful, just know that I was there not long ago. Very recently in fact, and in many many ways.

I guess that's all I'm really getting at. We've both reached this point, (me writing and you reading) because we want to know more. We want to learn more & question more. We want to better ourselves & in turn change the course of our lives as a whole. I mean, that's why I'm here. I'm not afraid to admit my addiction to self exploration and betterment, not just for me, but for this plane of existence itself. It's something that can, through it's own sheer will, change our lives completely, forever.

So if you're here for that reason, just know you're already ahead of the curve. Even if you're not, hopefully my story and guide can change that. How many views it may change is irrelevant, so long as these words can truly help at least one of you, I know they weren't written in vain.

This essence of awakening and the explorative nature to find out what we are, as well as who we are, is not as common as one would like to think. Some people never wake up. They live their entire lives through the eyes of a societal system. Never having the opportunity to say,

"Wait. There must be more to this. There must be more to me."

I am forever grateful that I did not have to live a life such as this. (Although how close I may have to it, I'm not sure any of you will believe).

So I just wanted to thank you. All of you. All of me. Every single face full of the same curiosity towards finding out who they truly are. You are the reason I'm embarking on this quest. You are canvas to my painting and you are as important a part of me, as I am part of you. With that being said, I hope you enjoy this bumpy, unpredictable ride that is my life, and what it came to teach me. At least so far. I know I have.

- Koi Fresco

A (Not So) Enlightened Youth

PART 1

A (Not So) Enlightened Youth

Chapter 1
Growing Up

Before we begin. I want you to know what this book encompasses. By now hopefully you've noticed that it's broken up into Part 1 and Part 2.

The first half of this book is my story, my life and my journey. The second half of this book is a simply a guide. A guide to bettering your life that came into existence through the trials of mine. Now one could easily skip the first half of this book and go straight for the guide. I wouldn't blame you. Why learn about me? Does it really matter? Well yes and no.

The guide itself does work in standalone fashion, so if that's all you want do not hesitate to skip forward to it. However possible this is, the guide itself came out of my experiences in life. That being said, I truly think in my heart of hearts that knowing my story, (however confusing and unexpected it may be) will help the awakening process within you when referencing this guide, occur in a much more fluent fashion. I'm as far from perfect as it gets and thanks to that, my story makes it much easier to understand just how much self change one can implement when truly surrendering to the true nature of reality.

It's never about where we begin, and never has been. What truly matters is when we wake up, when we understand just what we can open our eyes to, will make this path a most beautiful one to walk? Or will we ignore it? You tell me.

With that being said, you could say this, all of this, all began roughly 13.8 billion years ago. However my story is much younger. About 13,799,999,978 years younger to be, well, almost precise. The cosmic event that is my life all started 22 years ago in the state of Indiana. Not exactly the place most people expect me, or anyone now living in Los Angeles to come from for that matter, but it is.

This was the day Jackson Daniel was born.

Jackson Daniel? Who is Jackson Daniel? Now before we begin you'll have to realize one thing. Jackson Daniel and Koi Fresco are not the same person in the conventional sense. At least not any longer. But they were at one brief point.

For roughly 19-20 years of my life I was Jackson Daniel. For nearly the past 4 years I have been Koi Fresco. Both in name and spirit. You, the reader, would not have liked who I used to be. How do I know this? Because I don't like who I used to be.

The utter differences that exist between these two contrasting versions of me are something I want you to know. After all, it's the only true way for you to grasp the story to come, and the changes that lead me to who I am today.

Who Koi Fresco is.

Before we begin, let me be brutally honest and say writing this alone used to scare the hell out of me. I've always dread telling this story. Maybe it was my ego, my sense of identity or my inability to admit my faults, but I can tell it now. I no longer fear what was because it *was*. Meaning it no longer *is*.

Will it change your perception of me? I expect so. In all honesty I hope so. You'll judge me, which is fine. You'll probably be quite confused too. I implore you to welcome this feeling. The more you can truly understand who I was, the more this story and my methods of change may resonate with you, and hopefully help you enact this newfound life, before you run into the situations I most unfortunately did.

Early childhood was nothing out of the ordinary. Two parents, two stable incomes, one (sometimes annoying) little sister and all the toys one could ever want. I was just part of another classic American family you'd see sitcoms portray on T.V. You know, the ones with all the odd unnecessary problems that seemed to pop up? Yeah, something like that. At least from what I can remember.

Now my first memory wasn't a happy one ironically enough. See my grandmother had this pool built in her back yard. It was one of those pools that rose 3-4 feet off the ground to meet the height of the porch next to it. I must have only been 5-6 years old, but I remember losing a toy down the crack between said pool & the porch. From what I can remember, this was my first run in with attachment and loss, and boy was I attached to that toy.

No one could reach it after ten or so minutes of trying, I think I knew it wasn't coming back, and it never did. Maybe this had a subliminal effect on me, or maybe I'm just diving far to deep into that memory as I write about it. Who knows.

Even in my earliest days of youth I was a whirl-wind of hyperactive curiosity, and subsequent inconvenience for others. Nothing stood in the way of what I wanted to know, and what I wanted to do. My curiosity & outspoken nature very often got me in trouble than anything.

Maybe it was sitting in a bedroom with my sister as my parents fought. My mother fighting for family, my father fighting for money. Leading to a very quick and jolting divorce which may have originally lead tp not only my way of thinking, but my addiction to acting up without empathy. Maybe.

However at such a young age, it's hard to understand anything conceptually besides joy. Anger, sadness & confusion are all emotions that occur, but not that you can necessarily comprehend or understand in acute detail. So went my life. Next thing I knew I was living 2,000 miles away in Florida. In a town full of people older than my grandparents. The same place I would stay throughout my childhood, until the true shift in my life would occur. But this wasn't to happen for over a decade.

See I was never a "good" kid. Wait, let me rephrase that. I was never a "normal" kid. By normal I mean a kid who did what was expected. You know, go to school, follow directions, come home, play happily with my sister, go to bed when I'm told, and so on.

I broke nearly every rule I could during this pre-pubescent stage. I just wouldn't shut up or sit down. I was off the walls. What else can I say? So much so that I spend an entire night once with electrical nodes taped to my head while i drank Orange Soda & watch The Goofy Movie. I wanted to go to sleep, but wasn't allowed. Come to find out this was undoubtedly my first all nighter, which lead to the medical diagnosis that would in retrospect, change my entire perception on the Pharmaceutical and Psychiatric Industry. Simply for being an active healthy child, I was diagnosed with A.D.H.D.

A.D.H.D (as I'm sure many of you know by now) stands for Attention Deficit Hyperactivity Disorder. Bluntly speaking it meant that it my active nature was beyond control. Because of this "disease" I couldn't pay attention via sitting still in class or at home, and was overly hyperactive & easily distracted. I felt like just another curious kid who didn't want to accept what he was told at face value, but what does a kid know,?

The next step due to this diagnosis is what I like to think of as my childhood shift from playful curiosity & insubordination, to a version of me who functioned solely off the reactions I got from acting in malice & through rebellion. This step was due in part to the way my doctors saw fit to medicate my diagnosis. This step was having a hand forced upon me in which I had no control. A requirement to take a very potent medication known as Adderall.

Over the next few years I cycled through this medication like wildfire. Strattera, Ritalin, Vyvanse, and so forth. I was prescribed them all. I grew to hate this medicine with a passion.

I had no idea that the medication being force fed to me at the time wasn't just medicine, but an Amphetamine. A medical derivative of Methamphetamine, or Crystal Meth… So looking back my childhood consisted of daily dosing on a subsidiary of one of the hardest drugs known to man. Great doctors.

Now I understand that some people take it for fun, I learned that early on because I didn't. If I didn't take my medication every morning before school I would be grounded. For this I was pretty upset with my mother back then, but how could she have known? My mother is a goddess and one of the gentlest, nicest people you'll ever meet. It wasn't her fault for trusting a doctor. It is, (in most scenarios) the logical thing to do. But this medication did more harm to me than any good it could have ever done.

I started to become lost in my own head around the age of fourteen. When Middle School started.

The effects of this hard chemical cocktail in my stomach reacting with the chemicals in my brain took a toll. I started to almost lucidly daydream more than ever before. I knew my class schedules but I didn't care. I knew prior to walking into each class, that I had absolutely NO intention of even attempting to learn about the lesson at hand. Partially because my mind preferred drawing odd, random childhood graffiti, shapes and objects in my spiral notebook. And partially because as soon as I asked one question, I would follow it with another, and another, and another, until I found myself walking to detention with a referral slip in my hand because I just couldn't shut up.

My teachers hated me. Not because I was curious, but because I was either too curious, or too detached.

I could never just be. In the lesson. In the present moment. A problem that wouldn't be solved for years to come.

Knowing what I know now, it's hard not to be bitter towards a system which did it's best to keep me docile. After all, at that age amphetamines would take a heavy toll on anyone. Rarely was there a day for the next three years I didn't zone out in my last few periods at best. I slept, drew & day dreamt for hours on end until that last bell rang and I could finally find a tangible reason to muster up the energy needed to either go skate with my friends, or get home to pass out. I thought I was just weird and lazy. Now I know it was due to the effects of this medication.

Over time my rebellious side grew. I got better at, well, lying. Hiding the medication under my tongue, pretending to swallow it while dropping it down my jacket sleeve. I became more & more creative. Though slowly, I stopped taking it completely. That's where things really started to change. Unfortunately.

So where are we now? Oh yes, finally off the drugs. Finally. However to understand the sequence of events that what will come next, you have to also understand my personal life leading up to this. My hobbies, my talents, and what shaped my ego into what it was.

Outside of my reckless, legally drugged, insubordinate student self was a relatively normal kid. Sports were always a factor, from the time I could walk I played Soccer, Football, Wrestling, Baseball and Basketball. But over time it dwindled down to two activities worthy of occupying my free time.

Skateboarding & Football.

Forgoing video games, (which I still play to this day) these two activities became the essence of my existence. The only things that mattered in my life. They defined me.

Now I know what your thinking. Skaters & Jocks have a major stigma (with good reason) for being assholes. Self absorbed, acting as if they sit on top of the world. Luckily this wasn't me at first.

I was a quiet person before I hit high school. With maybe 10 friends total, one girlfriend ever, (leading to my first real kiss ever) I figured I would go into high school the same way.

Especially since the high school I'd be attending was in a different part of town, rendering me an unknown to the virtually two thousand other students.

Unfortunately I was wrong. See the year going into high school was 2008, and only two summers so far in my short 23 years of life changed me in the ways 2011 did, and the ways 2008 did.

So lets start with 2008.

Growing up in a white-collar town was all I ever knew as a kid. No crime, poverty or desolation. These were things that didn't make sense to me in virtually the same way that the

Buddha had never seen death or sickness before he left his father's kingdom.

Don't get me wrong, I'd stolen gum from convenience stores a few times and went skating in "no trespassing zones" but for the most part I was a reserved kid before high school.

My life was paid for in every fashion. When I wanted something I usually ended up getting it. This way of life was just, normal to me. I fooled around, but on a societal scale in my school I was more of a ghost than what one would call a, "popular kid " on any level.

My introduction to what you would call real life started my Freshman summer in 2008.

Like I said earlier, sports came naturally to me and always had. Because of this I found myself in a starting position on my team, which immediately put eyes on me. Within a week of practice I was making new friends. Along with this my confidence and ability to make large groups of people laugh grew with each practice. Before long this was translating into how I acted off the field as well.

My ego was growing at a rate I'd never experienced before. For the first time in my life I was actually holding conversations and making girls I found very cute laugh and smile. All while surrounding myself with equally confident friends who encouraged this behavior. The same way all good friends encourage each other. But this was still all new to me. Quite literally all of it.

Over the course of two summer months, I'd gone from a kid with friends ranging in the single digits, (a kid who'd only ever really kissed one girl and meant it) to a kid with over fifty good friends, while talking to two or three girls.

By the time school started officially, even though I was only a freshman, I went in knowing these four years were likely to be the best four years of my life. Which they ended up being…

Almost.

All went well as the year started. Friendships grew, our team got better, I started talking to a girl I really liked, and my self confidence kept expanding. Being just a Freshman, I wasn't yet up to the task of hanging out with upper class kids. I didn't feel cool enough yet because, why would they even want to associate with me? So I stuck with my core routine.

As time passed our team won districts and I ended up in a relationship with this girl. She was a cheerleader & was a 15 year old's definition of perfection. We complimented each other in almost every way.

So as this Freshman year came to an end, I was now a successful athlete in my class, dating a gorgeous and was well liked by my peers. The high school dream right? Yeah that's what I thought too. Which led to the development of some of the hardest habits I've ever developed. Habit's I'm still working on growing past even as I write this book today.

I went from confidence to arrogance. I stopped focusing on my personal progress and became addicted to proving how much more progress I was making than other people. I didn't feel like "me" if I wasn't better than everyone my eyes locked onto in some way shape or form. This habit was not only unknowingly toxic to me, but to the life I was leading because, like with anything in life, all good things will one day come to an end. But if you'd told that to me then I'd have laughed at such philosophical jargon and told you to leave me alone.

How blind I was.

I used to think good health was natural among all people. Simply because I was and have always been in relatively good health. Sure I'd gotten the chickenpox, had wisdom teeth pulled and contracted the flu a few times. But serious injuries weren't real to me. How could I in any way get seriously injured?

Couldn't happen. In my mind it was impossible. yet it happened. Now before this point, I was still what many would call a decently good kid. An asshole sometimes? Sure. But a good kid nonetheless. I followed some rules, got halfway decent grades & never snuck out or cheated on tests. I tested the water constantly but never splashed in without hesitation. So what came to occur the summer leading into Sophomore year was the true push into the downward spiral that would consume & dissolve the next few years of my life.

During football season my back had hurt pretty bad a few times. Not being a big person, you get used to being hit harder than others. You just deal with it. But it got to a point where I couldn't get out of bed or breathe because it hurt so much, this grew worse until my mother eventually took me to see a doctor.

I'll never forget the conversation I had when the X-rays came back.

"You've got Spondylosis" my doctor stated.

"I've, I've got what?"

"It mean's one of the vertebrae in your spine has slipped forward and is now pressing against another. This is due to a stress fracture in your Lumbar Five." he said.

Now, For those of you out there without a medical degree or extensive education on the Spine, let me fill you in. Essentially it meant that I had fractured my back. Fractured it badly enough that it caused a vertebrae (one of the bones in my spine) to shift forward and apply pressure to another vertebrae. Causing me extensive pain.

"How can we fix it? Season starts in a month or two and I need to be ready."

"It's not that simple." the doctor replied, "See, this is a relatively common occurance, but still a serious injury. There are only two ways of healing it. First, we can do surgery. We can clamp the bone back together with a plate, but taking this route means you can never play contact sports again in your life… Or, we can let it heal naturally, a process which can take a year or more to allow the spine to fully fuse back together."

So there it was.

A lose, lose situation. Great.

I wasn't sure which to pick, but after a few stressful days I decided my comfort level with surgery on my spine was close to zero, and instead went with the natural remedy. No sports, no running, no being active on any realistic level. Just play it calmly for the next year and you'll be fine. I thought I could handle this process, and that was my first mistake.

Remember, throughout this process I was involved in my first real relationship. Real as in my first taste of what only a 16 year old would consider "love".

To be confidential we'll call here Ana.

Now we didn't exactly have the most common views on life. At that age our bond had been formed out of the negative things in life more than the positive. We first met in 8th grade, stayed friends, and through one tough breakup she had in high school, we wound up together. It wasn't that she cheered and that I was good at sports, or any other predictable reason. It was because we seemed to be the only other people we each trusted with our problems and insecurities. We were best friends who decided to give a relationship a try. Which worked for awhile, but wouldn't work forever.

Coming into a situation of no sports, or physical activities, I really had nothing left to do but go home or go over to her house and spend the days together. She wound up quitting cheer, and we found ourselves well, quite frankly bored with life.

Which is odd at that age.

Prior to all of this, I had NEVER been the party type. I had drank a few times in friends garages when parents we're out, and experimented with marijuana only 3/4 times before my injury, and never really took much notice of these drugs because my physical abilities we're more important. She on the other hand, enjoyed them for quite long time and had been a fan of parties and experimenting with drugs. I knew about this, but like anyone in a relationship they wanted to be perfect, I decided to ignore it... And it worked, but only for a short while.

Chapter 2
The Crash

If you're young, what's to follow will hopefully help you from making the mistakes I did. If you're older, or have already made any amount of major mistakes, I'm sure you too can think back to the exact incident that started a vortex of trouble leading to rock bottom. A singular event that created a butterfly effect of trouble and chaos. Not just for me, but for many other people around the world who've made poor choices as well.

Some people die, some people never learn from these mistakes, and some people live their entire lives wishing they could go back and fix them.

What't to come is my mistake, as well as my salvation.

The first domino of trouble fell one late night party at a party in 2009. I'd been drinking and was only 16 but had still fallen farher to into the party scene with my girlfriend than I ever should have. The night was winding down and I had to go to the bathroom. I only opened a door, but ended up walking in on an entire world that would consume my foreseeable future. No I didn't walk in on my girlfriend cheating on me, or my friends stealing my stuff, I walked in on a group of people, (my girlfriend included) snorting pills.

I honestly didn't know what to think. Confusion overwhelmed me. They all looked at me like a baby who had no idea what was going on because to be fair, I didn't. All I could see were glazed eyes and soft smiles. They all looked so happy. I knew the pills were the reason why.

"Go outside! I'll be right there! Seriously go, you don't need to see this." Ana yelled trying to close the door on me.

But I was stubborn. If she could handle this, I could too. Maybe it was my longing for acceptance, or my insecurities on being left out yet again, but I wouldn't let it happen this time.

"I want to try it." I told her.

"Give me some of yours."

The way she looked at me, so reluctantly, I'll never forget it. You could see the guilt in her eyes for introducing me to this world, and although I was drunk and didn't notice it in the moment, looking back it's a moment that will never leave my mind. It was the look of someone who knows they've attributed to the death of innocence.

So she handed me pill. It was white and said *Xanax* on one side, with a big *2* on the other. The dosage was 2mg. A lot for someone who had never done pills in their life.

I swallowed it.

The rest of the night became a blur. A beautiful, warm, fuzzy blur. The happiest, most comfortable I had ever physically felt in my entire life. I didn't know it yet, but I was in love with them..

Even after this night life went on and as time passed, I did more and more Xanax. I started smoking more, stopped trying in school, started skipping classes to either spend the entire day with Ana, or to escape home where I could find peace and silence playing Xbox zoned out on these "bars".

It got progressively worse and as much as my friends tried to help me, they couldn't. I was too stubborn to let anyone attempt to give me advice. For the rest of the year the only through on my mind was to see Ana and buy Xanax. I was blinded by the effects of this drug. I had absolutely NO idea just how strong the grip it had on me was. If we got out of school and we were out of drugs, me and Ana fought about who should go get more. If we didn't have any before a party, we fought even more.

Nothing mattered without Xanax. Nothing. Not even Ana.

The relationship grew stale because of this and eventually physical contact was all that remained between to keep us together. Our friends knew it too. We began to fight far more often than we laughed. And finally, after months of screaming, crying and eventually cheating by both parties, I broke up with Ana. Now I was alone with my addiction.

I began doing the only thing I knew would keep me out of my room. I started hanging out with my dealers. I'm not sure if I ever even liked these kids at all, but I knew as long as we stayed friends, access to the drug I depended on wouldn't ever run out.

So I dove deeper into the rabbit hole still. Me and some other good friends began experimenting with psychedelic mushrooms, LSD, 2c compounds, and other chemical combinations that resulted in some of the most profound and incredible experiences of my life thus far. They began to lift me away from Xanax. It was like finding my life force that had gone missing months before. When I took LSD, my problems fell away and all that remained was me and the wonders of the cosmos.

These compounds actually got me hanging out with my old friends again, and got back near who I had been before pills took over.

We would buy supplues, we'd all take tabs or shrooms and just outside sit by the lake. We'd laugh and cry and talk about space and our dreams for the future. We'd party and smile and it began to feel like Xanax had only ever been a bad dream.

Ana. Pills. That entire lifestyle didn't make sense to me anymore. I was nearly over it. All of it.

Then James died.

Now New Years is usually a time of joy. A time for turning life around and starting fresh.

It ended up doing the opposite to me and the years to come.

On New Years Eve my friends George, Matt, James and I celebrated the new year. It was finally 2010. A new decade and a grand year to come. We got high, we laughed, and later on I said my goodbyes to Matt & James. Off they went. Just another year, another night with friends, not a worry in the world.

The next night I found myself at a party a few miles out of town, I was just about to head out when my friend Brittany called me. She was crying hysterically. My heart dropped.

"What's wrong?" I asked.

Three words. That's all she could get out.

"James got shot."

I hung up and immediately called my closes friends with James. They told me where they we're and I headed over. Since that day I've never driven anywhere near the speeds I did to get back in town, I was pushing 100mph the entire way, and when I arrived, found nearly thirty of my closest friends all sitting outside. Waiting on good news, bad news, any news really. Grasping for something to get us out of this confusion.

It just didn't feel real. My mind simply couldn't process what was going on. How did he get shot? Why? Who would shoot James? I was just with him the night before! There is no way this could have happened. But it did.

We all stayed up waiting on the news, and then it came.

James hadn't made it. My friend was dead. One of the nicest, happiest, friendly people I've ever had the pleasure of knowing had been shot and killed. As the details came out, it wound up simply being another case of being around the wrong situation at the wrong time. My friend was killed because of something he didn't do. Something he wasn't even involved in. He was killed for no reason whatsoever.

If you've ever lost someone this close to you, this suddenly, then you'll understand what happens to the mind when it occurs. If not, I hope you never have to experience such a range of raw emotions. Because if you're not ready for them, they can destroy you. Which is what they did to me.

How?

Because I just didn't *understand.*

Nothing made sense after James died. I was angry, confused, scared. I'd never known anyone in my life who'd died before and it frightened the shit out of me. I stopped sleeping. Picked up anxiety attacks and just felt all out guilty that he was gone and I was still here. That an innocent kid was killed due to the problems of thugs standing next to him. So I coped with myself in the only way I knew how at that age. I went back to what worked. Xanax. I went back to giving up.

The crazy thing about a drug like Xanax is the loss of memories. For nearly the entire year, and to this day, I really can't remember anything except the occasional party, girl, and trips to Miami to party with even more people. Eventually I got caught stealing an iPod in school and wound up doing community service for it, as well as being threatened with losing my license due to missing over 55 days of school during that year. Seriously. I was told by a police offer that I'd skipped roughly 1/3rd of the year. No idea how I wasn't held back.

My habit was so bad that following Sophomore graduation, I decided the only way to fix this was to switch schools. So I made yet another mistake, and enrolled in a Catholic School, (while already leaving the religion) in the hopes of getting my grades up enough to fix my GPA in time for college. But this only made life harder.

While I did have friends at this new school, I was still a black sheep. I wasn't religious, didn't believe in a god of any sort, and *really* didn't like following rules that made no sense.

I was constantly cited for insubordination as well as for questioning my teachers authority. While my grades did improve, I still managed to get myself detention virtually every week.

I've just never been the type of person to blindly follow rules. Especially religious rules. Especially religious rules that made no sense and had no direct answer. So three months before the end of that school year, in March of 2011 I was expelled.

Up until this point in life (and even now thinking as far back as possible). I'd never really experienced any truly lasting amount of individual alone time. Sure we're all alone for odd hours of the day every once and a while. But through being expelled, I was forced to take classes online, and thusly found myself alone virtually 12 hours a day. This in part was due to my mom working extended shifts and my sister still in school and sports.

A state of what I can only call craziness began to seep over me. I was weak, young and still didn't have a grasp on my emotions. I'd poured all my energy into drugs, girls and other forms of instant gratification on a daily basis just so i wouldn't have to be alone with my thoughts. Just so I wouldn't have to face my own mind, or truly recognize the nothingness I'd become. That would become evident soon enough.

From this point on the downward spiral of my life worsened. I continued taking online classes to finish the year but because of it, fell into a routine of secretly drinking or doing pills daily. Half due to addiction, half due to boredom. It was one hell of a destructive combination.

The months became a blur and before I knew it the month of May was upon me. A month that changed my life.

I was home, following the same basic routine as always, but on this particular day I desperately needed company. So I invited some friends over. There was a bottle of rum & some soda in my closet we intended to share. The last bottle I've drank since. My friends Kris , Melissa & Luke decided to come over after I invited them and we spent the next few hours progressively fading into a drunken stupor. Before we knew it, Kurt wanted to go home. We said our goodbyes and he walked out the door. A few minutes later he came running back inside,

"Its raining. Can you drive me home?" He said.

I already knew my answer, "No."

"Come on! Its raining and I'm not trying to get soaked, just give me a ride. I only live a mile away." he pleaded.

Now I won't lie, because the truth is I had already driven tipsy a few times prior to this, like a handful of teens do when given a license without proper guidance. But I was always alone and never with other people in the vehicle. Yet something inside of me knew when he asked me to drive that cold day, that I was far far too intoxicated to take anyone anywhere safely. So I resisted... Just not well enough.

Over the following few minutes my friend pleaded with me to take him home and, after becoming sick internally of this repetitive questioning, I did the only think I knew would make it stop.

"Alright calm down, I'll drive you home."

So we wound up with total of four of people in the car, as my other friends insisted on coming along for the ride too. Another mistake I made was allowing them to join us.

From this point forward I don't remember much. It's like looking back on a puzzle. Some areas of it are crystal clear, some are still as foggy as the day it happened.

I remember getting in my car, pissed off & drunk, wanting to get this over with quickly. By quickly this equated to driving far too fast just to get my friend home. We reached the main road, with a speed limit of 20mph, my car was already going double that and I had no intentions of slowing down. Then came the bend in the road.

Now in order to understand what happened next, you have to understand why I didn't slow down. Otherwise I'll look like a complete idiot, instead of a regular drunk one. This "bend" in the road was as close to a 90 degree angle as can get, yet it was still a very broad turn. You'd cut the corner and return to your lane once you'd rounded it. It wasn't just me doing this, (as I'd lived in the area for years at this point and witnessed nearly everyone do it). Ranging from kids my age to grandparents pushing 80 take the corner this way. So it was a normal, almost instinctual decision to make.

On a normal day with good conditions, taking this corner at 30-40 wasn't an odd thing. I mean it did exert a small amount of G-force upon you, but nothing major. Probably the same amount you'd get coming off a round-a-bout on any given highway. The problem this day, was the rain.

As I said before, growing up in Florida meant weather was unpredictable. You could experience weeks without rain, then get five days straight of torrential downpours. This took a toll on the roads. Because without rain, oils leaking from the bottom of vehicles create a build up on the road. Therefore when it rains after a long period of no rain, you're left with a thick, greasy coating sitting on top of the road. This alone is what leads to an increase in accidents, (mainly due to hydroplaning) where this layer gets between your tires and the groud. Creating a state of virtually no friction between the two. You feel more like you're on ice than pavement when this occurs.

This is exactly what happened to me.

The combination of being a drunk, pissed off 18 year old with a car full of people traveling around a sharp corner covered in excess amounts of water and oil could have only ever led to one outcome. Which it did. Disaster.

As I took the corner time slowed down. This I remember vividly. Looking back, I think me & Luke were the only ones who knew what was going on. Kurt & Melissa never made a noise or any indication that they had any idea what was transpiring.

The car started to slip. We were hydroplaning.

Hydroplaning isn't too bad if you can recover. But that sort of recovery requires space for error. This road had none, as it was lined with a massive cement wall, surrounded by bushes and palm trees. We were heading for both.

My mind took everything in as it occurred in slow motion. Maybe it was in a state of flow, or maybe I was just drunk and trying not to die. So I did the only thing I could knowing we we're going to crash, I tried to turn out of the way of the wall. Doing this worked, but still couldn't save us, nothing could. Then we hit the tree.

I don't remember hitting the tree, just waking up afterwards. What I learned later was that we were probably going close to 40mph and in an instant, came to a complete stop. I was buckled up, Luke was buckled up, but my friends in the backseats of the car weren't.

The impact knocked me out, but i still managed to hit my head on the window, which would leave a gash on my forehead requiring a few stitches. This impacted cracked the window and I pass out. Luke was unscathed too, but Kurt and Melissa weren't so lucky. In our rush they hadn't buckled up and the force of the impact threw them into the back of the seats in front of them. Fracturing vertebrae in both their backs as well as knocking them out.

The moment I awoke, adrenaline was already flowing through my body, and I knew that I'd messed up big time.

Immediately dialing 9-1-1 to report the crash and get my friends help. Before I knew it ambulances had arrived. We we're all taken to the hospital and on the way, my blood was tested. The result was a BAC far over the legal limit. Especially for an eighteen year old.

At this point I was still, in some ways, numb to what had transpired. My mind was probably in a state of denial, but all I could think was, "How is this real?"

"How is this happening to me? This is impossible. This can't be real."

But it was. And after being cleared from the emergency room, I was subsequently handcuffed, and taken to jail.

A (Not So) Enlightened Youth

Chapter 3
Solitude

I was a junior in high school when all of this went down.

I was supposed to be enjoying my time laughing, partying, applying to colleges and preparing for the future. Instead I was now a high schooler with two felony charges against him awaiting a court decision that would dictate where my life went, and for how long. Not exactly the high school experience one imagines.

Giving up crossed my mind hundreds of time over the year following my crash. When it all began I was facing 10+ years in prison. This was due to my friends being hurt, meaning the state had to press charges against me. This sort of time frame was quite literally, inconceivable, because of the fact I hadn't even been alive for two 10 year periods. Maybe killing myself was easier? Maybe running away to Canada or Europe was the way to go? After all I had (and still have) a very good grip on the underbelly of the internet.

If I really needed to, I could get my hands on a fake I.D.

Yeah that's what I'll do. I could get away with it.

But then what? What about my family, friends, dreams & future? How could this realistically work? Truth was it couldn't. So I did the only thing left, I started dealing with the problem the only way I knew how. I turned back to drugs.

Some people express their emotions freely. Some people have a significant other to confide in and share their fears and worries with, but up unto this point, I didn't. At this point I was in near constant isolation at home. But after the accident, I spent the summer with my family in Indiana, returned home to attend school and complete my senior year. I met a girl. Lets call her Emily. During this time my streak of isolation was broken and I found myself truly in love for the first time. My first brush with actual love. The selfless kind. For that I will always be grateful to her. Because without her ,I'm not sure I would have handled the situation as well as I managed, despite how much it weighed on me both mentally and physcially.

As I said, some people have others to confide in, to express their innermost feelings with, but I was selfish before this. I always had been in the emotional sense. Bluntly put, the idea of telling someone how I felt was weakness in my eyes. I'd been raised much like any normal male to believe masculinity took precedence over emotions. That whatever feelings lay inside me, no matter how badly they needed to be brought up and talked about even if only to help ease the mind slight, was being a coward. Men didn't do that. It was treated much like failing in a sense. Expressing yourself meant I wasn't really a *man*. So I didn't.

As my Senior year passed, I did my best to improve upon who I really was. Not change in the sense of stopping drinking, After all that was the only coping mechanism I had at the time keeping me from falling apart or running away. But change in the sense of doing my best not to get in trouble at school, and to just be, well, good!

Stay home. Avoid parties and social events. The works. This worked through isolating myself to my core group of friends and besides that, doing nothing but spend time on video games in my room, intoxicate myself, and re-assure my fears at night, (every night) that everything was going to be okay. That I would by some miraculous intervention of the universe, avoid jail time and be on my merry way to college and a normal life once again. Deep down though, no matter how much I masked it, the truth was that none of these things would ever come to fruition. I knew it, but wouldn't accept it. Denial was my best friend.

So the cycle continued. Go to School. Visit Emily. Head home. Get drunk. Fall into depression. Pass out. Wake up. Repeat.

The only thing impressive about this time in my life was how well hidden it was. Nobody, and I mean nobody knew what was going on in my mind or behind the scenes when my bedroom door closed. Just me.

High school came to pass meaning I'd successfully graduated. Much to my discontent however, we found out that Emily would be moving to Texas. There was no way around it. This too passed painfully, leaving me alone once again. Receding back into the darkness. Before I knew it, September had arrived and my sentencing date had come with it.

Now the problem with the legal system is that unless you are well versed in the law, you have virtually *no* idea what fate awaits you. On that day, just hours before sentencing, I still had no idea what to expect.

Eventually my lawyer found me and broke the news.

"They're offering 1 year in jail, and 1 year on house arrest." he said.

Now to most this must seem like a horrible deal. But to me, a nineteen year old kid, it was a dream come true. Especially when originally facing a decade. So I made a decision and in a somewhat bittersweet way, took his offer. Thus my descent into solitude took its final step. I was nineteen. I was a convicted felon. I would be behind bars for an entire year, and as far as I could tell, my life was already totally over. Because if you've never been to jail, (hopefully you haven't) here's how the process goes; First fingerprints, then paperwork, then a very violating physical, followed by medical examination, a change of clothes into your new outfit, (in this case a bright orange jumpsuit) and then being handed your essentials containing soap, tooth paste, a tooth brush, a bed mat, and a pillow. No more, no less. Welcome to jail.

My first day in, I was scared to death. I had up until this point, assumed jail was identical to the movie adaptations of it. Luckily this wasn't the case. Were there fights, gambling & thefts? Of course. But these were the rare occasion. Or, the norm if you were associating with the wrong crowds. This alone was my first true insight into the nature of what it means to be human. Jail is a place where animal instincts are more visible than anything I'd ever seen in my life. It was a spot on representation of what a jungle for humans would look like.

See in jail, people aren't trying to impress anyone else. You don't wake up and act a certain way to get praise, because in all honesty, no one cares about your self appointed status.. I found people to be more honest, more real and more true to themselves and their core values than I ever have before or since leaving that wicked place. Maybe it was because each person's ego was already shot. Everyone was locked up because, (like me) they had made a mistake and were now dealing with the repercussions. Embarrassing repercussions. So really, what would you be able to prove by acting cool or better than anyone else? Nothing at all. So no one really did.

Most people (myself included) assume jail to be a place of horror and unending sadness, but that isn't the case at all.

See when you live as you do now, you're probably in your room or on a couch, maybe sitting aboard a bus or plane, who knows. Regardless, you have plans and you have goals for the immediate future. Maybe it's what you want to do tomorrow, or next week, but the flip side is that you also have worries because due to this focus on the future. Every day of my youth included a few core actions. I would try to impress people, from friends to strangers. I would worry about grades, about relationships, and I would essentially live for tomorrow instead of focus mt awareness on the moment. On today.

Just think about it. We all do this. If you're reading this on a week day, I'm sure you've been more focused on how happy you'll be once the weekend rolls around. Vice-versa for those reading on a Sunday, dreading tomorrow because it brings with it a Monday. These are normal societal thoughts and emotions that we're raised with. We become so used to them, that we accept them as standard, when they *aren't*.

This revelation became clear to me within 2 weeks of being locked up. The notion of "plans" all but disappear, along with the worries of tomorrow. It was like a weight lifted from my shoulders for the first time in my life. I was behind bars, in a giant white cage with 40+ other men society deemed unworthy, but for the first time in my entire life, I felt liberated. In a most paradoxical sense, had caught a glimpse of what it truly meant to be free.

Adding to this paradox is the understanding that when you are locked up, time passes both quickly and slowly. It all depended on how busy you kept yourself, and how you deal with the concept of time itself. If you spend the whole day trying to sleep and watching the clock, time will pass exponentially slower than those who fill their days drawing, working, watching movir reruns on jail T.Vs or playing poker.

My first few weeks I tried the 'sleep through my sentence' method to no avail. So I began filling my time with work duty. Which was comprised of 1 six hour shift per day, that payed exactly $0 an hour. What a deal right?

However time which passed faster when working, so I did it anyways. It gave you a sense purpose in a place where you had none. Looking back I'm sure that contributed to how I view the world now too.

The crazy thing about jail that can really get to you is how frozen time appears. Not just for your future, but for any progress you may make inside those walls. Because even if you do, absolutely none of it matters until you're free again and able to rejoin society to prove your worth. This understanding was my first taste of my existence being wasted. Me, my essence, anything I could ever be, was at a standstill. I was decaying while my family and friends outside the walls holding me back made progressive moves to continue on with their lives. This became to me, the hardest thing I dealt with my entire sentence. How do I make up for this lost time? How do I catch up and make certain this year wasn't a total waste?

Truth was, I had no idea.

Days continue on at a seemingly slower pace and I continued on too. I work, worked harder, played poker, watched moves, played basketball and slept. That was it. I wasn't really learning from my situation so much as I was trying to tolerate it until my release.

Growing up I'd always been an avid reader. From fiction to non-fiction I read constantly in my youth, but fell out of sync with reading around the time high school started up. I still can't remember why I stopped, but luckily the joy of picking up and immersing myself in a book never really left me. I had just gotten good at hiding it. In jail, there are a LOT of books. And by a lot i mean hundreds of them, (at least where I was).

Due to being part of the working sector of inmates, as luck would have it, I was placed in the dorm housing the library. Convenient right? Except I was too busy pity-partying myself to care. I gorged myself on external activities all the while trying to push away my inner curiosity or focus. I managed to keep this act up for about half of my sentence before curiosity got the better of me.

With six months in, and six months to go I made my first trip to the library. Ironically, the first book that caught my eye wound up being the one that would set in motion, the long road home to finding my true self.

A (Not So) Enlightened Youth

Chapter 4
Overload

The book I picked up was called in elegant simplicity:

"The Tao of Pooh"

I don't know why I picked it up. Maybe it was the fully red cover of the book. A very sensitive color to the human eye. Or maybe it was because I resonated with the stories read to me as a kid about Christopher Robin, Pooh & his friends. But oddly enough, I did not pick the book up because it was written about The Tao, or Taoism. Because quite frankly up until that point I hadn't really garnished and interest in those ideas.

Buddhism had been something I began to study briefly and philosophically before incarceration, but not so much Taoism. Funny how one book can change everything.

The book, (through references using Piglet & Pooh) depicts The Tao. Which is essentially the way of all things. Ultimate truth & being. The flow of everything in existence being all encompassing and connected. Is-ness. So much so that any attempt to truly describe "The Tao" is impossible, as words are limited themselves, whereas The Tao is not. The Tao simply *is*. This concept decimated my mind and ego like nothing before it ever had.

Quite frankly I didn't know how to process the impact it had. It was a rush of anxiety, mixed with a feeling of liberation and happiness. Was I really free? Was I simply part of one massively complex & conjoined entity that was existence?

Yes. I. Was.

The studies I had come to know through Buddhism touched on this, but I must not have been paying enough attention to the existential philosophy of those teachings at the time. My focus was just centered on the path it game me the chance to follow. This simple and short book revitalized that understanding for me. The same way jumper cables are needed to start a dead battery, I needed a book like this to jolt me up and say,

"Hey you! Yes, you! Y are free! Stop running from the truth! Embrace it! Love it! Make the most of it!"

So I told myself I would. It was time to make the most of my confinement as well. I checked out four more books on eastern culture and philosophy and started reading, as well as taking notes. Notes that I still have sitting in my apartment to this day.

The more I read, the quicker time seemed to pass, and with it, the weight laying upon my shoulders began to fade too. When you're taking in philosophies dealing with the cessation of suffering, existential realities and the understanding of how politics & religions all revolve around central power structures, everything in day to day life starts to look a lot less important.

Now not less in the sense you may be thinking. All things do still exist, and on a very prominent level at that. However you begin to see it all as a game, a game that for some reason, people devote their lives to. This alone well, this begins to seem crazy the deeper you think about it. As if everyone on the planet signed up for a massive role playing session that lasts an entire lifetime. One where only a select few realize that they don't have to actually follow the rules of the game at all. That they can play the game, but not to complete missions, and instead simply to explore and enjoy and have fun.

This was my first glimpse through life's foggy veil, into the unknown, untouched realm of ultimate unending choice.

I was on the cusp of understanding the potential liberation I had at my fingertips, and like anything in life, it takes more than one glimpse of what can *be*, to truly grasp what *is*.

From here on out the days decreased and my release date got closer and closer. Although I had spent the past four months consuming as much knowledge as possible from these books, I wasn't quite at the point I could laugh off any problem or conceive of a logical way to explain or accept me feelings. So slowly but surely, the anxiety bug crept back into my life.

You might now be thinking, "But Koi, you're about to be free. You'll be home soon. What could possibly worry you about that?"

Trust me I understand where you're coming from. It's a logical and natural way of thinking. Yet life isn't always logical itself. See when your behind bars life is easier than ever. It's like being a kid again. You're told what to do, when to sit down, when to eat, etc...

Quite simply you don't *think* about anything you do, because there's really no need to when you're part of such a rigorous schedule. Nothing is going to happen outside of this schedule, so why would your mind even imagine alternate scenarios?

Living on the outside world, or better yet living in real day to day life however is the complete opposite. Taxes exist. You must fund work. You have to go buy groceries, get gas, talk to family members and constantly fix small problems that come up out of nowhere. You deal with curveballs from the moment you wake up to the moment you go to sleep. They never stop coming. That's what makes life so fun! It's unpredictable. Jail life however, is very predictable. Which turns these curveballs from fun, to frightening.

So after a year of no curveballs, you start to really fear them. You get to a point of not wanting to have to deal with them ever again, but when you're free, that's unavoidable. It scared the life out of me knowing I would have to face them again. The main reason was due to what I had to deal with once I went home. Because for another year, living on house arrest would the foundation of my life.

It's a simple concept. Stay home unless you have permission to go somewhere. That's all it is.

This was the last major leg of punishment for my mistake. I would simply have to stay home, work a job, volunteer somewhere, and after twelve months I was free to do as I pleased. Much like all things in life that can present themselves as straightforward though, our inner fears and insecurities can destroy this notion of simplicity all together, which is exactly what it did for me.

Although the rules you must follow are relatively simple, the process itself is not. You can violate house arrest in this scenario very easily and when that happens, it's back to jail. How easy is it to violate? Here's a small list of things that count as a violation:

- If you don't answer the door when an officer knocks. (This mean any hour of the day or night. 24/7.)

- If you have any drugs in your house. (For me this included drinks such as beer and wine.)

- If you get home late from work or if you leave too early.

The list goes on. Essentially you have to be the definition of a perfect citizen. That is what was expected from the judicial system, and that was what they look for in me.

When I was finally released in September of 2013, I was not only excited to finally be home and with my family, but also very frightened that I would commit some small mistake and ruin everything. My biggest concern was missing a knock at the door.

Due to living in a house with multiple rooms, playing video games, watching movies and sleeping often, the anxiety that slowly built in the back of my mind over missing something as small as a knock on the door began to drive me insane. It's such an easy thing not to hear! How in the world would I be able to tune my ear to my front door 24/7? What if I was in the shower? What if I was sleeping? Could they really violate me for that? Yes. They could, and they would given the opportunity.

So although I was home, my mental state had begun to degrade far beyond any level it had reached while behind bars. Funny how life works that way.

The lack of sleep brought on symptoms of insomnia in me that I didn't know existed. I stopped going outside. Stopped sleeping except in short 30-60 minute bursts. Practically replicating an polyphasic method of sleep. I was burning myself out and it didn't show any signs of stopping.

Now I'm naturally skinny. 140lbs is the most I've ever weighed, but at this point in my life I was down to 110lbs and due to a major lack of sunlight I had regressed to a pale silhouette of my former self. I spent the first few months of freedom doing absolutely nothing but inviting girls over for nothing more than physical pleasure and a faint amount of conversations. I even began to take inappropriate pictures with some and posted them online as if in a way to impress people.

All in an effort to simply draw attention to myself, though looking back I can't even conceive of how this would have made me feel better. It ended up only tearing me apart more. I was alone. I was paranoid. I could feel myself slipping. I really thought I was going crazy.

Looking back, this was the worst life has ever gotten for me. As far as the future goes, it's highly unlikely no matter what happens, that I'll ever reach such a low and dark state of existence again.

Four months into my house arrest I was prescribed Clonazepam, otherwise known as Klonopin. A drug many use to get high, but in my case, to help me sleep. I was worried about addiction becoming a problem again but I knew without sleep my body would be far worse off than it would in a state of addiction. Slowly but surely it began to work, it was hard to accept it, but I needed it.

I wanted to save up dosages and get high of it so badly, but I wouldn't allow myself to. I had to get better. I had to fix myself and I had to finish up this sentence and get on with my life. I was weak. I had to make myself stronger.

Chapter 5
The Transition

The Second Catalyst in my life was fast approaching. Oddly enough, it wasn't a physical thing or person, or anything else that would edge this snowball effect in my life the wrong way. It was the birth of me, as I am now. The true me.

There are two versions of each of us I believe. The person we want to be in order to acquire material goods, impress people and boost up our ego, and then there is the true version of us. Who we really truly are at our core.

My entire life, from a popular kid in high school to a felon in jail, I had clung, even if just by a thread, to this original and shallow version of myself.

But after twenty years of life, I simply couldn't lie to myself any longer. It's not that I didn't know the other me was there. It's just that suppressing wholeheartedness was a natural reflex. As natural as breathing or eating. This itself though took effort to do so. A small amount of effort to hide it yes, but effort nonetheless. In order to change I had to simply be who I *really* was at my core. Hiding could no longer be an option. Much like going on an adventure to another country or having deep philosophical discussions with a friend, my goal was to discover not a place or thing, but myself.

The first thing to bring me into this light was music. Singing, rapping, playing ukulele, (not well, but still). Even helping my friends produce beats. These were the main things I did to pass my time on house arrest. From this art form I got very good at it. Good Enough to book shows with my friend, travel and play. However since I couldn't go with, he performed without me. Music was my therapy. My first true love. Something that, (at the time) I planned to do with the rest of my life.

It allowed me to relax. To work, make music, and proceed to spend the rest of my free time learning. Music was progressing on a constantly aesthetic scale. Watching more lectures, taking more notes, reading more books, on and on and on with no end in sight. Education was at this point in time, second to sound. Music was first. For this I will always be thankful for the role music played in my life.

When you begin to master a craft that evokes not only a physical stimuli such as the way music does for your ears. But also a mental stimuli such as those found in the levels of joy and confidence music brings with it, by the time you've finished your daily work/sessions you still want to do more. You don't want to relax, or sleep, or be lazy. Music, at least for me, made me want to better myself. Thus I began to slowly do so.

Originally I wanted to make progressive style hip-hop. The poetry and activist nature of this genre when portrayed correctly (see: Del the Funky Homo-sapien , Nas, Mos Def, Taleb Kweli, etc...) can change the ways we see the world. So in a way, this was in itself, hinting to my future as a teacher, only at this point i wanted to do so through sound. Sort of like education through music based poetry.

I began to produce with a mutual friend while living at home in Florida. Day after day, our content got better and day after day, the future looked brighter to not only me, but the impact I imagined I could have on the world. Since the age of 12, something inside of me, something that was part of my core makeup just *knew* I would be do something to make a change. I had no idea how, when or why, but could always feel it. Something important. Something that would be in some ways, unforgettable. Something that would make others smile. Now after all the problems, all my failures, I sort of felt like I was on the right path… The only real path for me.

This notion began to quell my anxiety. Now, when not making music, I could focus all personal time on growth and development. On my ever-growing addiction to knowledge, and so I would. Now you might be asking, "Koi, what made you want to learn so much? What compels you to chase new information?" And that's a hard question to answer. Mainly because the answer is almost to simply. That's how I am.

I grew up as a son to a mother who was a teacher, a grandmother who has also been a teacher, a father who with his friends built a successful multi-state business, as well as a grandson to a grandfather who ran his own farm for his entire life until he retired and sold it. So in the sense it all boils down to the ever debatable topic of nature vs. nurture.

I grew up around independent people. Curious people. Even if we disagreed on what was worthy of being curious towards. Two of them taught, (and by default made me realize the importance of asking questions and staying curious) while the other two we're fully independent and relied on themselves to solve any problem they faced. Creating an atmosphere around me centering on the importance of individuality.

Ask your own questions and solve your own problems. Don't automatically rely on others to fix or perfectly explain *anything* for you.

So from this my mind probably molded and emerged with this odd combination of extreme fixation on not only independence, (which most of us fixate on) but education as well.

It wasn't enough for me to be my own person. As far as I was concerned, I wasn't my own person until I could answer not just mine, but other people's questions and help them thusly. This didn't just emerge at twenty, it had been with me my whole life, I just didn't have the reflective ability to see it.

In school when being taught a lesson about, say, World War II, sleep was more important. Yet when I got home I found solace in watching WWII documentaries for hours, followed by another odd hour of surfing each and every WWII Wikipedia article I could find.

The problem wasn't a hesitancy to learn, which had always been my guess as to why I couldn't find the urge to focus. It was the simple fact that I wanted to teach *myself*. Not simply be another student to a teacher. I want to be a student and a teacher. Two sides of the same coin. Two pieces I never put together until now. So it goes.

This understanding, this realization into why I acted and reacted in the ways I did changed me. The way I hope the second half of this book may help you change yourself. When you understand why you tick the way you do, an internal liberation of sorts occurs.

For some this liberation never comes to fruition. For others it doesn't happen until forty or fifty years of age, during what many consider their mid-life-crisis. Mine occurred at twenty.

The exact date? I've since forgotten it. Although going back I'm sure it was around the middle of 2013. More than three years from when I'm writing this book now. I can understand how to some this isn't exactly considered that long of a time. But all is subjective when it comes to time either way. And for me, a lifetime of change has since transpired in these last three years of life.

As 2013 ended and 2014 began to pass, my vision cleared more and more with each day. No longer did I spend my time solely on music, movies and regressive forms of attention, but instead found myself returning to the young but sturdy roots I had discovered in jail. Books. Followed by documentaries,, lectures, meditation and yoga.

This was all essential to my growth and because of this, I decided that to not make time for them would only lead to self destruction. This road was new, scary and confusing. Yet I had to keep on it, if I really wanted to improve my life. There was no way around it.

I started eating healthier, (not yet vegan but healthier regardless) because up until twenty my life was full of candy, soda and fast food. Breaking this addiction came to be harder than I expected.

Also I had went on to spend the residual money I had left for fun on about 10 or so used paperback books. Ranging from Richard Alpert to Richard Dawkins and other authors in between.

Variety was key after all.

College was a part time thing for me during all of this too but after completing only one semester, I dropped out. Deciding I would rather learn from courses that interested me, online. Mainly so I wouldn't have to pay. Thankfully Stanford, Princeton. Yale & Cambridge all had YouTube lecture channels to solidify my choice.

From this spawned countless hours of intense personal focus. My personal favorites being Philosophy, Social Psychology and Particle Physics. What we can think of, why we think of these things, and how we think the universe works. Symmetry. Symmetry. Symmetry.

So here I was. Creating music, racking my brain as heavily as I could afterwards, falling asleep and repeating the same steps again when I woke up. I absolutely loved it. However one problem still persisted, how to get out of Florida?

Now for those wondering, I was grew up in two small cities. One called Mt. Vernon, In (5,000+ people) and another city called Naples, Fl (20,000+ people). Like anyone from a small city or town can tell you, places like this create a black hole of sorts when it comes to leaving. Even to this day I remain amazed at just how rare it is for people to leave the places they consider home. Most of my childhood friends are still in these cities too.

Working 40 hour a week day jobs and hating it. Granted some of them, including a few very close friends are working their asses of to escape like I did and for that I will always love and respect them. But as for the rest of them, leaving home? Well that's just not an option. Maybe it's stubbornness. Maybe it's fear. For me though, leaving was a high priority on my list of things to do once I was eighteen since before I could remember. Where to though? That was up for debate.

Originally I had wanted to move to downtown Miami. In fact, I tell most of the people I meet that I'm actually from Miami. Only because:

1.) No one knows where Naples is

2.) Naples is only about an hour from Miami

This makes it easier for people to understand the vicinity of the area from which I originate. Going there was the goal for quite a while, but like most of us know, income often winds up having the final say in what we do, as it did in my case too.

Miami was, simply put, *far* more expensive to live in than I had originally anticipated. Even with adding roommates. Thus my ideal future somewhere by the beach on the Atlantic Coast ended, and my journey to the west began.

Chapter 6
An Understanding of Awareness

Think of the United States.

Now if you're familiar with the states themselves, think of which one you would attribute the word 'paradise' to. Did you pick California? Because if not we may have very different definitions of the word.

To me and what I'm sure are millions of people, California is the epitome of, "the place to be". It's the most diverse state geologically. The state with the highest GDP. It has medicinal marijuana, (although I don't smoke this is still a major selling point to a large sector of people) and the largest port in the Pacific Ocean. Oh and of course; The home of the stars. I once read somewhere that if California were to secede from The United States, it would have the 6th highest GPD of any country in the *world*. So it's safe to say the place is a powerhouse of potential in virtually all forms.

Potential was all my life was about at this point. The future, what I could do, what I could accomplish, etc...

The only thing which worried me was if Miami was to expensive, would Los Angeles be as well? This was the million dollar question. It was nearing summer 2014 now and I was only months away from being free to chase a normal life again. The one thing I knew though was that under no circumstances was I going to attempt doing this from my home town. I had put up with the place for my entire childhood and now that adulthood was blossoming within me, I knew staying home would only hold me back or get me in more trouble.

I had to leave and get far away at that. Los Angeles being roughly 3,000 miles away, was the perfect solution.

Music was why me and my friends wanted to move originally. In fact, the kids I came out here with are, (as far as I know) still pursuing that dream. But for me even without music something inside me knew that no matter what I did in life, I must be somewhere I can interact with likeminded souls.

Somewhere I can connect with tons of other creative minds and meet the right people, not just for my craft but for my life. A place with community. After a week or so of planning, I made the decision that would change my life once again, for the rest of my life. I was moving to the West Coast.

Money was the first obstacle to overcome. As I tell anyone who ask's me how I got out here, saving money is key to effectively making any major transition in your life. When rent isn't and issue and food isn't an issue, life is much moe noticeably easier to flow and adapt with. Change as well. So from the odd jobs I'd worked as a kid (which wasn't much at all) to the savings bonds I had been fortunate enough to acquire from grand parents growing up, I decided to cash in my chips. I wound up with about $6,000 to my name. Not a penny more.

Luckily though this was far more than what I needed to pay rent and find a job once I'd settled in to Los Angeles.

The green light was lit. All systems were go. The journey to L.A was cemented in stone. It was going to happen.

Funnily enough, the night before leaving the East Coast for good, I had a full on breakdown. My last breakdown to date. I wasn't regretting the move, or doubting my ability to do it, I was just a mess of extreme nerves and confusion. Would I be able to make it? Would this city chew me up and spit me out like it does to so many others? Would I be able to function again in society now that my jail time and house arrest was over? One million questions, zero answers. Much like life itself. So I calmed my nerves, forced myself to meditate, (although it didn't do much to help at the time), and went to sleep.

When I awoke I hopped in the car with my incredible grandparents, who then drove me roughly 10 hours north to New Orleans where I had booked a cross-country train ticket, spanning 20+ stops and 2,000+ miles. All ending in Los Angeles.

The limit to these trains was set at 200lbs of total luggage. So that's what I packed. An entire life, from birth to twenty years of age. All stuffed into 4 small suitcases. It was a surreal but still an overwhelmingly joyous thing to experience, as I'm sure many who have packed up and moved off to college or elsewhere can hopefully understand.

I kissed my grandparents goodbye, and with the slide of one door, I was on my own. Really on my own. For the first time in my life, the rest of my life wasn't going to be decided by the court, or by my parents, or as a reaction to my ignorance. Instead it would be the direct product of what I put out into the world. I would be forced to work harder than ever, to put in more effort than ever before, and any failure from here on out would be on my shoulders.

The ride itself was beautiful. The scenery kept me up and sitting in the observation cart of my train for most of the grueling 48 hour trip. During this time I kept my headphones in with an endless stream of Alan Watts and Jidda Krishnamurti to keep my mind on it's toes. What a wonderful weekend it was on that train.

Now, in a video game we have the option to restart at any time. I'm sure we all can attest, (or at least I can) to wishing we could use such an ability once or twice in life. Unfortunately life doesn't give us that option. We must change, adapt and morph constantly to what is occurring in this moment, and deal with what has transpired. Starting over is almost never an option placed at our feet.

Yet somehow I still felt that moving was in some odd way, acting as a reset button for my life. Not just a fresh path, but a new me. Like a snake shedding it's skin for the first time. Who I was on this train ride, and who I had begun to grow into over the last two years was not who I fully *was*. I had grown in a way most never do, in part because of my obtained experiences via experiencing such a devastatingly unique situation. It had been a wild ride of life altering experiences, to the point where my friends, the people I had spent an entire lifetime growing up with, seemed like nothing more than memories.

We'd all grown apart at such a rapid rate that my change was, almost forcibly accepted by both parties. Even to this day, from my former self to who I am now, I've only kept around 3-6 friends throughout the entire process. These few souls are my brothers and sisters. True family. And they too have slowly adapted over time into their own uniquely progressive lifestyles. Much like the one I was falling deeper and deeper into.

When I finally stepped off that train, a truly new me had finally began to emerge. This in turn would bring a fully new life with it. I could, (and would) point my energy inward. My focus was not only to master my mind, but to understand the planet and universe I was so enthralled with being a part of. The true me was beginning was beginning to recognize itself. What a joyous moment it was.

As that train ride was coming to an end, I came to one final conclusion. I knew, deep inside my myself, that I wasn't "Jackson Daniel" anymore. That person had withered away.

The person who grew up and took pride in that name and the reckless actions he was involved with was not the same person who sat in an observation cart flying across the Arizona Deserts on his way to California with tears in his eyes due to the raw beauty of the landscape around him. That person was gone. The individual who remained what someone new, and he needed a name. After all, as an adult, why shouldn't one be able to call themselves what they wanted? Not just what they wanted, but by whatever combination of sound the universe wills one to subjectively go by?

So I started thinking…

Art was key to my life at this point. I loved art in all forms, from painting, to drawing, to music, to education and even cinematography & photography. Love for all these entities was a driving factor behind the passion forging my quest for change. Through this research I discovered this kanji "恋".

It translated to 'Koi' in English. Which, (roughly) translates to what we would call, 'passionate love'. Arguably the deepest form of love one can have for anther thing. Both selfish and selfless. Understanding but dedicated. Koi. Koi. Koi. Koi. *Koi.*

I knew from the moment I spoke the syllable out loud to myself that I would go by that name for the rest of my life. Explaining why is difficult because the definition of the word wasn't the reason Koi stuck. It simply *felt right.*

I had grown into Koi. And I would continue to grow as Koi.

The last name I decided upon was strictly to pay homage to a major inspiration in my life. While many people would come to know me as Koi, almost all people in my life from this point on still knew Daniel as my last name too. After all, attempting to change one's last name legally not only cost's a lot of money, but takes a lot of time. Along with this I was still new to utilizing social media and creating work online. In all honesty I just didn't want my real name out there for the world to see. It just didn't feel safe. Or maybe I was just scared someone would find out about my past and judge me on it, instead of what I put out into the world now.

Instead of all this hassle and worry, why not make up a last name I thought? Use it as a sort of stage name for anything you may do as you go forward. This is what most people do online anyways. It's actually quite rare to find anyone who uses their full legal name at all. An odd phenomena, but one I could sympathize with. So I picked Fresco.

Why?

1.) Plainly put; To honor a great man. Jacque Fresco. Creator of The Venus Project, a man who's spent his entire life attempting to help humanity as well.

If you haven't heard of him, I highly suggest you look into his work, vision and life in general. He's the type of people we need. The type of person who wants to create a tangible world of love and harmony.

So there I was. Reborn if you'd like to call it. Koi Fresco.

From that day forward, (and still to this day) what I decided to go by, began when I stepped onto that platform at Union Station to begin my life in Los Angeles. That is exactly who I would grow and cultivate myself as. A flowing entity trying to harmonize with the totality of existence around me.

Not as the ignorant, material, selfish, drug addicted failure that the prior me had grown comfortable with being. Someone addicted instead, to helping others. Someone addicted to knowledge, and most of all, to the betterment of myself and the world in any way I could make possible. It was time for a true change. An understanding of true awareness.

Now I could go on from here, about the past two years since I've arrived in Los Angeles, but from this point on my YouTube videos document more of my personal progress than writing a few more pages in this book ever could. If you're reading this book wondering, "What Videos?", type this into your computer search bar: (https://Youtube.com/KoisCorner). Other than this, I'll keep it simple.

I moved into a place with some friends from home. Started working on music and even got a few shows. It was fun to do, but it still wasn't me being my true self. Yet I still didn't get the sense of synchronicity originally created from what had grown to make me happy. Not even the simplest things such as posting positive/thought provoking tweets, (which at this point had helped me create a following on just Twitter alone) had done once before. So If there's one person I have to thank for jumpstarting the movement I'm working towards now, It would be my friend Lindsey.

Coffee has always been my vice. Always. Maybe it's my way of staying away from drugs, or maybe it's just a reminder that I can jumpstart myself safely, without really damaging my body and mind in the process. Still now writing this, I find myself drinking coffee most mornings. Lindsey as it so happens loved coffee too, as well as making a living off the incredible, controversial platform known as YouTube. Now let me be clear, before this conversing with my new friend over coffee, I had *never* even remotely considered making YouTube videos.

Not one single time.

How did I plan to make an impact and teach people that way? Who knows. I sure as hell didn't. Maybe I would just write books as I am now, or maybe I would goto film school and create documentaries. Which I still plan to do. Well ot film school, but documentaries.

However Lindsey changed that. She'd been familiar with my tweets and expressed that I should try turing those 140 character blurbs into videos.

"No Way." I said, "No one will ever watch that type of stuff."

"Yes they will!" She reassured me, "Just try it out."

As I'll get to further on in this book, you'll see me reference quite often to fear. Fear is the innermost factor as to why change in any form fails to become a part of peoples lives. When I went home from this discussion, and decided to seriously attempt the idea Lindsey had given me, it absolutely filled me with fear.

What if nobody watches the videos? What if they do watch them and hate my content? How can I find a way to do this effectively? What if they think my writing, or acting, or editing sucks?

Hundreds of 'what if' scenarios raced through my mind. I could have easily succumb to them. I could have never even attempted to make a video, but one other thought came to mind too. What if it works?

What. If. It. Works?

This was all I needed. I had begun a new life, was a new person with a new name and new ambitions to change myself for the better. A person who had moved across the country to embrace these opportunities and now that I had one would I let my doubts or fears overrule me? Would I really let them stop me from chasing something truly meaningful? No. I simply couldn't allow myself to. So I didn't.

I spent the money, bought the equipment, and created my first video. What a wild and beautiful ride this decision would turn out to be.

My first video went live in December of 2014.

Koi's Corner was born. My new life had begun.

Now if you're reading this, (regardless of age) and you don't know what you want to do with your life, trust me when I say I absolutely understand. It took me twenty one years to discover what sort of life fit me. What I wanted to spend my time on this planet doing. With this knowledge let me also say, when you do realize what you want to do in life, it hits you like a ton of bricks. I like to call it 'mini-enlightenment'.

This occurrence took place for me shortly after posting my first video. Everything clicked. Everything shifted and my perception realigned itself in real time, with such force that I had to sit down to take it all in. This feeling was magical. Almost mythical and divine in nature. It wasn't a decision I made or brooded on either. My body, my life essence itself simply *knew* this is what I needed to do. Teach. Help others. Grow with them as a community. So that's what I knew I had to do.

Over the next odd year I wound up quitting the music entirely, and moving into my own place. Life has been nothing but productive and positive towards me since these transitions took place. I spend my time currently hiking, reading, writing, creating videos for anyone who might want to watch them and as always, learning as much as I can. All while attempting to maintain a social life although I'm not too good at it.

So here I am now. It's mid 2016 as I wrap up this small story about myself, but the bigger story held in the second half of this book is much larger, and far more important than anything you've read here thus far.

In all truth I didn't want to even write about myself, but I felt it was necessary. I didn't want to simply present you with a new way of finding yourself and changing your life without some perspective on me. All of me. After all I am no guru. I am no savant and I am no more important for devising this method to come than you are for learning it through this book.

My life and actions forced me to discover this method. My experiences are the sole reasons for this awakening, however new it may be. Because of this rapid and effective change in my life I felt it necessary to open all the doors I have priorly wanted to keep hidden. Only in this way could you visualize me. Who I was, imperfections and all, transitioning into the person I am now.

Not perfect, but better.

Anyone can awaken this awareness. Anyone can change their life in this way, but not everyone needs go through the destructivity I did. We can all awaken right now. With or without letting our 'demons' get the better of us before we do.

Mine almost won. almost. Quite frankly I don't want you or anyone who picks this book up to ever reach the lows I did. Hopefully what's to come next can prevent that from happening.

With that being said, lets get to it.

PART 2

Chapter 7
The Guide to Finding Yourself

Let me be clear when I say this method is not an end-all method. Reading the rest of this book alone will not by default result in a magical new life for you. In fact it may not work at all.

On the other side of this coin however, the methods I found conductive to enacting changes in my life may change yours too. It may just lead to a complete overhaul of your mind and body. A revolution in discovering who you truly have the potential to become. I guess what I'm saying is that right now, before we begin, throw out your expectations. Go ahead. Get rid of them.

You've read my story. You've metaphorically seen what I what I went through to get here. However one fact still stands; that was my path, not yours. Going into this guide with any bias whatsoever is only going to set you up for failure.

This doesn't mean not to use this method. It simply means to keep an open mind and interpret these guidelines in a way that fits your life best. After all, these methods are more so realizations than anything else. Things noticed in the moment, as they occurred.

Only after much self reflection was I able to see exactly what these realizations were, and therefore translate them into a visual path to be used in daily life. Essentially these pathways unfolded subconsciously within me. Only recently way I even able to forge them into words.

Order is another factor when considering this path. The steps to follow are set precisely in an orderly fashion that fit *me* best. Therefore, remember that you are not experiencing the same path. From this, feel free if need be, to change the order of these steps if all else fails. Do I think this will be necessary? Not so much. But it never hurts to let you know they can still work together, even if out of order. That being said I truly do think the order presented here will be the most effective. After all, accepting a new life (Chapter 11) will make much more sense if undertaken *after* you master your logical and emotional states (Chapter 10). Things like this will be likely to confuse you if the path isn't followed. All I can say is mix them with caution.

View it like a sport. First, master the fundamentals. Once that is done you are free to tweak and change the game at your leisure, but if the fundamentals aren't fully grasped, the game won't ever really be yours to change.

Along these lines you'll notice some of what I say may sound familiar. That's because it is. Much of what I learned and discovered can also be viewed in other philosophical pathways in life. From Empiricism to the Eightfold Path, and all ventures in between. What does this mean? Essentially I'm telling you to look into other paths, not just mine. Read mine, take it to heart, use it to change you life but do not view it as the only one you'll need, because it most likely wont bey. I follow my path dearly, but I also follow The Eightfold Path, and have some very deeply rooted existentialist views pertaining to the nature of existence.

We are complex creatures. One simple guide won't always be enough to cover all the ways of thinking we have, or things we want to do. So it never hurts to cultivate multiple practices through patience and time, instead of just one.

Granted thay you may, after much research come to the conclusion that this path IS the only path you intend on following, and that's alright too. After all, there is no right or wrong path. They are just paths. Any one path is no more or no less important by default. Your subjective interpretation of the path dictates it's morality. effectiveness and importance. Nothing else.

Much like a movie, these paths (and our viewpoints on them) tend to reflect our own lack of understanding more than our grasp of what that said path really is.

The majority of us view movies as cheap entertainment, but the trained eye only ever views them as potential works of cinematic art. This difference lies strictly in the eye of the beholder. To follow this guide under the guise of ignorance & laziness will only lead you off the path entirely. Only when you understand just what created the path, goes into the guide, and from this enacts change, can you truly begin to follow it in the manner originally intended.

This guide will be broken down into distinct categories, followed by methods pertaining to making them work together, and finally, presented in a way to give back to those around you. All in an effort to help them find the light that lies within them as well.

With that being said, lets begin.

A (Not So) Enlightened Youth

Chapter 8
The Unknown

We have become a scared species. A species trained in the art of learned helplessness. Darkness petrifies us. Death looms over us like a shadow that never fades, no matter how much sunlight there is. We run from what we don't understand, as well as shut out what we do understand if it confuses us or forces us to questions our perception of life and all that encompasses it.

For such a technologically advanced society, our inner emotions, (at least in their current state) do more harm than good. But why is this?

One answer sums this up. Our near unlimited access to information. Something never before seen or experienced in the history of humanity, and quite possibly the universe.

After all, the average twelve year old with a laptop has access to more information, both scientific and theoretical, than the entirety of humanity did just fifty years ago. Think about that. In just sixty short years we've transitioned from computers the size of football fields, to computers that can fit in our shirt pocket. It truly is a new age of existence and progress. A turning point in our rise as a species.

Yet knowledge is a double-edged sword. Only when wielded correctly can it be used and understood in a method that doesn't harm the one holding this beautiful weapon. In this aspect it's easy to see on a global scale, that not many know how to weird such a sword the right way.

Why is this? Why is knowledge now so often equated to fear? The answer is hidden in plain view.

In the past our limited access to information meant limited concepts that could exist within the mind. If you didn't have any way of knowing what global warming was, you quite literally couldn't worry about it. This is because the concept did not yet exist in your mind. However this is just one individual example. Now multiply it by a few billion. What are you left with?

You get a world of learned chaos and fear. A world of people with more questions than answers. And when we have more questions than answers, it tends to scare us. The essence of, 'what ifs' in life are unavoidable with the way we are brought up currently.

What if I fail this test? What if I lose my job? What if there is only nothingness after I die? What if my spouse is cheating in me?

The list goes on with no end in sight, and no answers to cease this worrying nature rooted deep within. This is where we must begin our journey to finding ourselves and redirecting our lives.

We must embrace that which we do not know. More specifically, we must learn to fully embrace the understanding that, for as long as we live, there will be an endless realm of unknowns presenting themselves in our lives. That to dwell on them, instead of redirecting our energy to what is occurring here and now, will do nothing but hurt who we truly are at our core. Who we have the potential of becoming.

To dwell is to attach. To attach is to create unnecessary suffering for ourselves. This suffering is what's known in Buddhism as *Duhkha*. This Duhkha can range from physical suffering to mental suffering, and all areas of life in-between.

Most commonly, this suffering is due in part to the specific attachment of wanting things to remain a certain way, or have them go back to a way they once were. Humans have this odd, paradoxical, almost innate tendency to long for things which do not change, and resist that which does.

Why do we want things to stay the same? Because it's something we know. Something we understand. Something we are comfortable with. In fact it's engrained within us. Due to our long lifespans, compared to other animals on this planet, we have a skewed perspective of our time here on Earth. This as it turns out, not only presents itself as a blessing, but a curse.

Because change in human life is so gradual, we tend not to notice it. It happens so subtly that even small, constant changes can be easily overlooked. We pluck our grey hairs, we get surgery to maintain our youthful appearances, and we let deaths of loved ones devastate us. Even with the full understanding that hundreds of thousands of deaths are occurring on a daily basis.

Why is this?

Because we've become addicted to lying to ourselves.

We must stop this coddling of the mind. It will only weaken us. We must wake up to the true nature of being, and see that the concept of sameness, (on both a physical and mental level) does not exist. It never has.

Accepting this notion is the first pillar of awakening and the foundation upon which this entire guide is based. Without a strong foundation, the entire structure to come will crumble. So how can we come to embrace this unknown nature of constant unending change? How can we effectively see, in our daily life, this stream of creation and destruction in a way that is conductive to personal change? Easy. By following the stream. Because life is just that; an endless, eternal stream.

Think of the universe. Now think of it's beginning. How did it occur? From what science shows us currently the most probable answer is known as The Big Bang. However even this occurrence wasn't the beginning of *everything*.

The Big Bang simply created, from what we can tell, space and time. So tell me, what existed before that?

Do you see the trend in this line of questioning? It becomes nonsensical. The answer does not exist. If this occurrence created space and time, then asking what happened before it is akin to asking; What lies north of the north pole?

Can you ask the question?

Yes.

Is asking such a question pertinent to growth, let alone the confusion that follows when you understand the question itself is unanswerable?

No.

This is life, from what existed before The Big Bang, (if anything did) to it's creation of space and time, to the formations of Earth, continuing on to this exact moment during which your eyes pass across these words, is all one existential stream of change! Creation *and* continuation. It always has been. We've simply mastered the art of fooling ourselves into thinking it isn't.

This is what you must see in each day. You must see that all is change, and always has been. Why? Because change, by default, creates unknowns. Questions that can't be answered and answers that lack questions. This is a significant factor in progress.

Why?

Because acceptance of the unknown dilutes the fear of it.

Imagine you are falling from the sky, with no recollection of why. At first, you would be overwhelmed with fear.

Will I survive the fall? Where will I land? What caused me to fall?

All natural questions. All lacking answers.

Then imagine during this fall, you look down and see a giant pile of pillows. Along with this you notice that your falling velocity has somehow slowed down to the point where you *know* you will survive the fall.

At this point you still have all these unanswered questions from before in your mind. The difference is, that you now know the asking of said questions was irrelevant! How so?

Because when looking down at safety, something inside tells you that you will be alright. When this occurs you begin to embraced the unknowns, forget the purposeless questions, and simply focus on the current existing outcome, surviving the fall. You immerse yourself in this state of flow. You simply accept what is.

Could you still die upon impact? Yes! But how would you rather die in this situation? In a state of complete fear and anxiety, with an endless stream of unanswerable questions running through your mind? Or would you rather go out in a state of serenity and peace? A state where unanswerable questions cease to phase you, and the only thing that does is where you are in this moment.

This is the art of embracing the unknown.

It is the art of accepting this universal truth of life. That we cannot answer all the questions we ask ourselves, and to stress over them will do nothing but harm us. It is akin to fearing the dark, or fearing death. It is a fear that resides solely in our imaginations.

When you truly see life as the never-ending stream it is, you begin to laugh at these unknowns. You begin to see just how odd it is that people let their lives revolve around these fears, and because of it, never truly experience what it means to live.

Death is but part of this stream too of course. It will come, just like brith came. So why worry? How will that enact an awakening in our lives? The truth is, it won't.

Science now shows that nearly everything, from stress, to cancer originates within the mind. Worrying truly can kill us. So why do it? Because on the opposite end of this spectrum, science also shows us the benefits of ceasing these negative thoughts. Mindfulness and positivity leads to better mental heath, weight loss, confidence, an increased ability to complete tasks, realignment of hormones in our body and many more things. both biological and psychological.

This all begins with quelling the anxiety of 'not knowing', of letting these unknowns rule over you. Next time you watch the news, look at what you see. Death, poverty, terrorism, etc... Yet what you do not see is the news on life saving discoveries science is making, or the heroic stories of the average citizen saving a life or stopping a crime. Why? Because we live in a society that thrives on this fear. A society rooted in oppressing the individual to the state of making one scared of their own existence. We do not learn on T.V that we humans now live in the most peaceful era in human history. Which we do.

We do not learn that slavery is at an all time low in recorded history, or that humans are living longer, healthier lives on average than ever before. This isn't simply forgotten by accident, it's swept under the rug on purpose.

Because in our current state, it is much easier to control lives with fear, than with optimism.

You *must* wake up from this as I did. When you see that life, (despite the corruption and propaganda we are flooded with to convince us it's awfulness) is actually truly beautiful, and that we are capable of quite honestly anything, a natural surge of empowerment begins to rise from within. With this you can truly begin to hold the keys to your own destiny. All you must do is let go and see the truth.

Upon doing this, you'll notice a detachment to those around you. Remember that this is natural, and that you cannot allow the stagnancy of others to hinder your personal progress. If all the most influential people around the world held back on their dreams and changes in their lives, simply because a parent or a friend didn't make an attempt to change theirs at the same time, the world would be a much darker place. When my journey began and I truly let go of those around me who decided not to pursue a path of personal growth, i lost the majority of people I'd known since childhood.

This is natural. This is expected. So you must be ready to do so when embracing the unknowns that self awakening may create. You simply cannot expect another person, in a much different mind state, to understand why it is you're deciding to pursue this journey deep into the self. Do your best to explain it to them in a manner they may come to understand, but do not let their lack of understanding or resistance stop you.

Unknowns create a cognitive bias within the mind. We can see this in what's known as, 'The Ambiguity Effect'. A psychological trait which was discovered in 1961. What this test showed was that people tend to make choices based on what they already know.

Say for instance your boss gives you two choices:

A.) He offers you an $h8 raise

B.) He offers you a chance to pick a number from behind his back. If you guess correct, you will receive a $16 raise

Which would you chose?

If you went with the $8 raise you'd be among the vast majority of people. After all its a logical decision to make. It is a decision you make subconsciously. How? Because even though option B gives the opportunity to make more money, it has a property of uncertainty to it. Uncertainty is something humans highly dislike.

To make the decision of going with option B is to forego this instinctual nature of accepting only what we already know, and to venture into the land of probability. You must harness this thrill of embracing the unknown side of life and attempt as best you can to stop automatically going with the option A's. Why? Because selecting option A creates no change.

When picking A, all you get is exactly what was expected. Nothing more. You accept it and go along with your day. No thinking required. Only when choosing option B can you have a growing experience. Regardless of whether you're wrong or right, you still gain the ability to reflect on the situation, and use that information to gauge the way you shape the future. You gain perspective. Something option A will never give you.

Each day we learn. Each day questions will be answered, and others will remain unanswered. As time passes your mind will ease into this new transitional method of thinking. A state of mind capable of endless curiosity & endless yearning for knowledge. A mind in love with the confusion that surrounds this existence we experience in each moment of each day.

A mind that embraces that which it does not know.

Chapter 9
Balancing Act

Fragility is an inherent quality of life. We can see this when we look at flowers, clouds, small insects, and so forth. Rarely though do we attribute this fragility to ourselves, and even lesser still to the state of our mind. We have quite a hard time bypassing our egos and admitting these fragile mental states exist simply because we are raised with the notion that to admit our faults, is to admit weakness. This is as far from the truth as one can get.

The concept of a perfect mind does not exist. Even an enlightened mind has to mold and cultivate itself into a personal, yet unbounded universal understanding of nirvana.

More-so, even when these states have been reached, many of those who do reach them return to prior states of mind in an effort to teach their methods to others. After all, in Buddhism, to reach Enlightenment & not return to society and teach your ways is heavily shunned. So on a technical level we are all not only mentally imperfect right now, but also when reaching the highest state of thinking and being. We are urged, across all cultures, to return to our imperfect mind and spread knowledge. Quite the Catch 22 isn't it?

You might be ask why I'm telling you this. A right question indeed. Let me be clear, I promise I'm not trying to dissuade anyone from reaching an awakened state. Quite the opposite.

Because the state of mind we reside in shapes the world we live in. A pessimist will always find problems in a perfect day, and vice versa. So where you stand when you are alone with your thoughts, and how you react or control yourself with others will directly influence how you view all that occurs around you. It has the potential to distort even the clearest of messages, on the sunniest of days.

The mind is not a simple thing. The mind is not something we can simply 'hack' and feel better instantly because of.

It takes effort, cultivation, dedication and an inclination to help ones self on a higher level than ever before. However we can, subjectively, break the mind down into what I find to be the two most important, (and ironically enough) misbalanced aspects of the mind in general. Logic and Emotions.

A battle of opposites embedded within the mind that we all experience in each day of our lives, even if we don't know it's occurring. Logic is structural. Logic is a rigid method of reasoning and critical thinking void of emotions or opinions. Logic is a method of understanding what *is* in the most empirical sense of the word, versus what we *want* to be true. What expect to be true.

Without logic, science could not and would not have even remotely advanced to the stage it has reached today.

Along these lines, logic, via philosophy was the precursor to critical thinking, existence, morality and social psychology. Without it, these things would never have been born so to speak. These things rely on logic. We as well rely on the ability to distance ourselves from any given situation, and instead analyze it from a third party perspective. Though this line of thinking is rarely taught in our current era of education. We must understand a viewpoint void of personal intentions, if we ever intend to hold a viewpoint consisting of universal intent. An awakening does not occur when one shuts out the truth of what is, but when ones embrace them. Logic lies at the heart of this equation.

Along with anything in existence, regardless of how entangled the mind and psyche within us is, we must find balance. This is where our emotions, which can be far more difficult to master than logic, comes into the equation.

The problem begins with understanding that most of us are consumed by our emotions. To be quite frank however, this is rarely a fault we bring upon ourselves, but a fault of our cultural upbringing. A fault imposed upon us in the way we were raised.

Technology has advanced quickly in the past 100 years, but the cultural normalities of humans still has some catching up to do. This is expected, but we are moving into an era in human history where this must be corrected in real time. In the now.

At our core, no matter how much we try to push it away, the facts remain; We are animals. We are part of the animal kingdom and just because we sit atop the pyramid in terms of evolutionary success and development, does not mean we are by any means perfect because of this. The weak grip we have upon our emotions are a testament to this in their own right. If you can understand that we have unavoidable biological instincts that likely won't fade away any time soon, then it should be equally as easy to envision your emotions as the most visual aspect of this spectrum. If you still can't see this, just look at your pets, or any video of an animal in the wild online.

Wild animals get angry and fight. Humans too get angry and fight. Cat's waiting for food meow, which is their version of complaining. Much the same as we humans do when put in the same position. This is why it becomes so easy to personify and mirror animals emotionally, and why we empathize with them, instead of with say, water or with a piece of concrete.

We exhibit near identical emotional reactions in almost all facets of our life to our family in the wild. Yet the one factor that separates us is our capacity to *notice* these emotions and correct them. Our intellect, if applied correctly, can create a new state of mind. A state where one's emotions don't rule their lives, but instead are ruled by said individual, in every moment of every day. How emotions are expressed and treated no longer becomes an overwhelming, uncontrollable aspect of life, but a well trained strength.

This road to control lies with logic.

The concept of logic, many would argue, is not an inherent attribute of personal awakening. This means, (in layman terms) that logic is not absolutely necessary to realizing the true nature of the self, or of what simply is. This is true.

However, this guide is not a guide to enlightenment, nirvana, or any concept of 'awakening' as a stand alone entity. Instead this is, (as I've stated earlier) a guide to finding yourself. Right here, right now. Only from that point, can one use this pathway to eventually find higher states of being.

When it comes to understanding one's self, the mastery of logical thinking is and has always been a necessary stepping stone. Why you might ask?

Because you are, (most likely) not an aesthetic monk.

If you have access to this book, regardless of how, it was most likely acquired somewhere either online or in stores. This itself was done via a currency exchange, representing the fact that you have the money to buy this book, which you did. This also means you most likely live in a first-world society, as do I.

An aesthetic, hidden in the jungles of Myanmar has *no need* for an in depth understanding of logic along his/her journey because their life does not require it! He/She will likely not be, nor ever agree to participating in group discussions, debates, social interactions, relationships, income, and so forth. All things we experience every day, even if not intending to do so.

Our lifestyles require the ability to debate, to hold our own, have discussions, and reason correctly but compassionately. All the while not letting our emotions override and ruin whatever concept may be at the core of said discussion.

A problem that a vast majority of the population lack the ability to control. So lets start with Reasoning.

Reasoning by definition is the act of thinking logically. The ability to draw an understanding of what you are learning, or perceiving, without letting your natural cognitive biases and/or personal interests get in the way. This is why when someone is freaking out over something that, in actuality is not worth freaking out over, you'll often hear one say, "Oh, be reasonable!"

After all, if a fly makes it's way into your room, and you freak out, you are acting very unreasonably. Logically, what can a small bug, with no painful defensive mechanisms do to you? Nothing.

What does it's presence do to ruin the situation at hand? Again, nothing. The correct response, and one we must learn, is to be reasonable in this situation. Simply accept that due to the nature of the situation, and the fact that the probability of a small fly causing any real damage is essentially zero, that you should do the only reasonable thing left. Relax and leave the fly alone. This act of correct reasoning breaks down into two halves; deductive and inductive reasoning.

Most people tend to think inductively in all facets of life. What does this mean? Let's look at a popular example known as "The Gambler's Fallacy".

Say you go out to a casino and decide to play roulette. You place 50 chips on 0 (the only green spot on the entire wheel and just 1 of 38 total spots) but end up winning! That's amazing!

So you decide to double up, place 100 chips on 0 and you win again! There must be a pattern to this right? So inductively, you decide to place all of your chips on 0 again, as there is an obvious pattern occurring. Right?

Wrong.

This is the problem with inductive reasoning. It is the idea of specific, unique occurrences, being generalized as something normal. You won twice on the same spot, so your mind tends to generalize this as common, therefore fooling yourself into thinking you can win again on the third spin. But in reality this isn't the case at all.

Each spin is completely unique. In no way shape or form are any of the Roulette wheel's spins related to the prior ones. But emotionally we are attached to this idea of such occurrences being interconnected, when they aren't.

Is the universe an an interconnected entity? Yes! On an atomic level it very well is. But on a mathematical level of chance & probability in regards to a casino game, it is not. It cannot be predicted. Each occurrence is it's own unique thing, and each conclusion is it's own as well.

This is why inductive reasoning can harm our personal progress. It leads us to assume that because something has occurred in the past, it may happen again for us, or to us. The destructive nature of this mental construct is visible on a sociopolitical level.

People will see one or two Muslim extremists in the news and assume all Muslims are violent. This is not the case.

People will read a horoscope, decides their personality fits this somehow mystical format of very basic psychology, (even when disproven by science) and decide that it is fact. This is not the case.

People will do a drug, fail to form an addiction the first time, and therefore convince themselves they are impervious to addiction. *This is not the case.*

We must *not* let this method of thinking control our lives, as it so easily can when we ignore it's presence. Instead we should move towards a much more progressive, logical & awakened method of thinking.

Deductive reasoning.

Deductive reasoning is essentially the polar opposite of inductive reasoning. It is the act of taking the obvious, the expected, and the already accepted facets of life, and instead of allowing them to simply exist as they are, its no thought involved, doing one's own research.

Regardless of what your mind assumes the outcome will be. This process of analyzing each situation as it arises, instead of assuming it will function the exact same way it may have in the past, eventually leads to the art of forming your own logical conclusions based on what you discover. Free of personal wants, biases and expectations. Mindfulness.

Think about when you were little. We all thrash about, huff, puff, and become impatient about every little thing we didn't instantaneously understand. Yet whether it was a teacher or a parent, a voice of reason would come into the picture to calm us down. This figure would attempt to explain the situation *as it actually* was! In that moment! Not how we assumed it was.

We must cultivate this ability to understand everything going on through a critical and excited lens

.

I remember at a young age when I got in trouble, my dad (though I rarely saw him) would sit me down and print out spreadsheets on how to improve the situation I was in.

Talk about a business-minded individual. However as one continues to grow, it seems relatively visible that being an adult does not in fact mean knowing the answers to everything. It simply means being able to support ones self with the concept of potentials.

Many *many* people who lack critical thinking and logical ways of approaching problems can do this. Logic is not necessary to daily life, nor an aesthetic way of life. But it is to ours, so we must make it a priority.

As we go about this process of weening off inductive reasoning, and focusing our mind on deductive thinking, it becomes far far easier to notice the attachment plaguing the majority of any given population.

You see thousands of people upset about traffic, yet they *are* the traffic! You see people mess up *once* on something and quit entirely! Instead of simply thinking critically and trying new routes to complete their tasks. Why is this?

The idea of letting common, everyday things ruin your complete state of mind is due to a critical failure. A failure to relax, to breathe, and to analyze the current situation logically, as it is happening, in this moment. When you can do this, arguments turn into discussions. Stress over waiting in lines turns into a practice of mindfulness. We can use this time to plan the rest of our day, or to google questions we are curious over, instead of stating still, letting anger consume us.

This is what being logical looks like. Logic goes far deeper than reasoning, this is true, but reasoning is at the core of decision making, and thus interlaced with the path we will come to create. Yet this is still only the tip of the iceberg.

After this chapter concludes, continue your research farther and deeper outside this book. It never hurts to try…

But what can hurt us, in fact the only thing besides physical pain that can do any damage whatsoever, is caused by our emotions. We must spring-clean these emotions. Correct them, tidy them up, then integrate them with logic in a way that makes us free to simply be. Not just with how we feel but how we think.

Recall back into your past as far as you can. Do you remember the first time you experienced emotional turmoil over something? I certainly do.

I was probably 3-4 year old and as I said earlier, (pg.11 of this book) I was deeply effected at the loss of my favorite toy. It devastated little me because I held it dear. I attached to the very idea of the toy itself. My emotions controlled me, and rightly so, as it's very uncommon to find a toddler with the ability to control their emotions, let alone an adult.

Why is this? What about emotions can lead to them making such visceral impacts on our lives? They limit us yet they strengthen us. They close us off to ideas and opportunities yet also allow us to let go and express ourselves fully if need be. Quite the case of 'pick your poison'.

Except it isn't.

The crux of civilization in it's current state is what impedes the majority of people from reaching their true potential, and from coming to understand who they truly are at their core. How? Because we are raised to ignore our emotions. To hold them in and bundle them up and forget about them.

Next time you're around a parent with a small child in public, watch how they react to crying, whining, or any emotion that takes them even just a few steps outside the peaceful state of mind they want. Do they listen to the child? Rarely. Do they try to barter, reason, or explain why the child cannot get what they want? Maybe, but not often. What I've noticed, especially reaching the age now where friends are starting to have children, is that a large amount of parents will do whatever is necessary to cease any from of distress coming from their kid. If a child cries, even if for no reason, we coddle them and tell them to quiet down.

What we don't do is listen. We don't explain to them that they can't always get what we want. Instead we've done the opposite. If a child cries, now more often than not, they get what they want. So long as it calms them down. This is creating a learned behavior that while not taught with ill intent by the parent, can absolutely devastate the mind of an individual if continued into adulthood. Life is not something that simply hands you rewards for complaining. No, life is something that in actuality, laughs at our complaints and forces us to actually work for what we want. Even going so far as forcing us to change our perception of the problem entirely, so that we no longer see a need to complain. We either move past it, find a solution, or let problems engulf us.

Whining, worrying, complaining and crying will get us nowhere. Not in childhood. Not in adulthood.

I never noticed this type of action, (although I was akin to it for much of my youth) until I started working full time jobs. To me, I was being paid to complete a task that I chosen to take on. Because of this there was no real room for stressing over it, nor for picking it apart. Yet some of my co-workers had a different view.

Day in and day out one in particular would complain about the pay, about her hair, about our dress codes, about wanting to get a new job. It never stopped.

The more I listened, the more I wanted to ask her why she was so adamant about vocalizing these views, yet do nothing to enact them. She never asked for a raise. She never asked if she could alter what she wore even if only a little. No, she simply chose to stress over nonexistent problems, without ever once attempting to formulate a solution and apply it to them.

This is the world we live in. A world of people with the strength to consider every bump in the road a problem, but without the will to go around them, or to find a way over them.

To truly master the emotional side of who we are, to discover what we are capable of at our core, we must not cling to these thoughts. Instead we must be aware of when they arise and simply *notice them*. Do not dwell. All you have to do is be aware of why you are thinking this way, and the problem will either present itself with a solution, or fade away.

This is where mindfulness comes in to play.

Mindfulness is arguable the easiest concept to understand, but is for some reason not taught often enough in schools.

How do you feel right now? Happy,? Sad? Tired? Regardless, just from reading that, you are now becoming aware of how you feel.

This is Mindfulness.

Now ask yourself why you are feeling whichever emotion you are noticing. This too is the art of mindfulness.

Mindfulness is simply the art of being *aware* of our current conscious state. Emotions included. It is simply understanding that they exist, and why they have lead us to this state of mind. Awareness of the present moment in it's totality.

This is Mindfulness.

It's hard to believe something so simple can be so pivotal to self growth and transformation, but it can. When you can understand your emotional state in the current moment, from a third party perspective, you start to gain new insight into who you are. It's like having two different lines of thinking at once. Hard to envision, but easy to see once you begin the practice.

Through mindfulness we see our emotions as fluid in nature, much like everything in life. Therefore we become better at understanding their reason for existing, in accordance to ourselves. The more we practice, the better we get at controlling our emotions in all facets. But we can go a step further in my view and implement logic into the equation of mindfulness.

By implementing logic into our awareness we not only allow ourselves to *see* our own state of mind for what it truly is, in each moment, but gain too the ability of retrospectively analyzing it. A methodology that can help us in some senses, chart our emotional state. Therefore gaining the ability to see just what exactly arises in the situations we react to. We also through this induction of logic discover how to phase out the unnecessary stress, anxiety and sadness from life itself.

When applying our strengthened ability to use deductive reasoning we can now for the first time use skepticism to analyze each situation on a level that flows much deeper than a strictly emotional state of being shows us. This ads in the cultivation of self growth far more than one would ever gain from mindfulness alone. We gather the insight as to why the situation itself may matter. From our friends to the weather. Even things as simple as what we may have ate today.

If our body itself isn't in the right state, (due potentially to poor diet or lack of exercise) then many other factors without logic would go unnoticed as well. And currently do go unnoticed to the mass majority of people on this planet.

When we learn to look at ourselves as flawed, as a sort of trial run or test subject. We can begin to see waking up as being born anew in each day. Each time our eyes open, we have the potential to be reborn in that moment. Through this we truly gain the ability to let go of what we 'think' we should be.

This opens up the doors of empiricism. Of self-experimentation. We can question our own minds, test new methods of living and approach even the simplest of situations like we never have before. Most importantly, we can come to master our own mind in it's totality. A feat I believe is necessary to achieve before attempting to travel down the path towards attaining nirvana, or forgo the essence of self entirely.

After all, only by fully understanding both sides of this coin, can we ever claim to know who we really are.

Chapter 10:
One Story, Two Sides

Each of the steps taken prior to this are of a selfish nature.

How so? Because we need to awaken. We need to change our lives for the better. This is by definition a selfish act. To accept existential curiosity and to balance our state mind we must step back from the whole. We must recede from our place in this group scenario and analyze our unique self. Only by doing this can we return to the group, in an effort to impact them as well.

This next step is one of awareness. One that forces us to see that the more we master personal practices, the more detached we may feel from those around us. Without even noticing it one may start to box others in, even if done subconsciously. Now judgement is a natural part of human evolution and survival. What we do not perceive as akin to our own progress, we hesitate to surround ourselves with.

You can see this across all platforms or progress, education, and popular culture as well. Vegans will sometimes scoff and attack those who eat meat. Members of an athletic community mocks and looks down upon the obese and overweight. Those who harness what society considers 'good genetics' in turn convince those who look differently, that their failure to use the products they use is what has results in them looking how they do. In a sense we fall into a state of tunnel vision when we begin to truly master a craft or understand the depths of a subject.

This is where the next fork in the road to finding one's true self begins to take fruition not just in the mind, but in the communal world as well.

It is the seeing of not only the tunnel, but what creates the tunnel, and what lies beyond the tunnel.

To fully understand ourselves we must *see* the totality of each situation. Not just our bias viewpoint, but *all* viewpoints in each moment we experience. Daily, culturally, and so forth. We must internally analyze our judgement of how we alone understand each moment. Through this method of thinking we gain the ability to see what created it, as well as what the other side of each story may be.

Why is this important? Because we as humans are imperfect.

Our state of mind is not always correct, empathetic, or understanding. We are naturally rigid and dismissive at times. We live with defensive instinct and to be quiet honest, simply wouldn't have reached the present day without them. The world was and still is for virtually all species but our own, ruled by judgmental instincts. But it doesn't have to be.

We have now grown past the point of relying on fear to guide us. Instead, we have achieved milestones once thought unfathomable. But we are far from finished. Have you ever noticed how humans have the analytical ability to reach the moon, but lack the compassion to care for those who hold beliefs different than our own?

We outlaw the most basic of things from love, to personality, and even the freedom of conscious alteration. We act on a global scale, like children.

This is what we must come to understand. You alone must see why this occurs. You will need to forge a vantage which takes a vast amount of time to accomplish. One I myself still work on each day of my life. Cultivating ones self is not a race, but an intricate work of art.

Let's begin with a new way to view each other and each day.

Think of this moment, right now, as part of a video game. A game which saves each night when we go to sleep. Now imagine yourself as quite the experienced player. Not a master, not a professional, but someone who has a very good concept of the game and how it works. Got it? Good. Lets continue.

Now imagine there are level markers that floats above your head at all times. A bright, blinking number that represents the totality of skill sets you've acquired so far in life. In accordance with this book you may be at lets say, level 40 out of 100. 1 is a newborn baby, 100 is an individual who has reached a fully enlightened state. The more you help other and yourself, the quicker you level up.

You the reader, recently becoming aware of the need to better yourself, your emotions, and to laugh at unnecessary fears, have began to level up quickly. And to the untrained eye you would seem a pretty skilled player.

Now imagine you run into a new player you've never seen before. Like a stranger on the street in real life. They look different, they act different, and they don't quite grasp the impressiveness of the game itself. You look up, and see their level marker is only at 18.

You can *see* from their level of progress alone, that they quite literally *don't know* as much as you do. Their perception of understanding, (from their own mind to the world they inhabit) is not yet on the same level as yours. Maybe they still find fear in questions, or get irrationally upset at small things, however the fact remains that they are simply a few steps behind you for whatever the reason may be.

Would you scoff at them? Would you seethe with anger at seeing they are so many levels below you? No! Of course not.

You wouldn't do this because you already know the only purpose of the game is progress. The same purpose that exists here and now on this planet in real life.

So now knowing this, why would you ever get upset in real life? The truth is you shouldn't. Because real life is about process in the same way this fictional game is. Yet most people still do get upset at small things like this. They simply cannot stand the notion that another person lacks the understanding they have.

This skewed viewpoint is what distances people and teaches them to harbor animosity towards others of a 'lower level'.

You the reader however, are only leading yourself astray when doing this. To judge without attempting to understand both sides of a situation is to walk backwards.

This must change. From this point on. Including tomorrow and years into the future, try to view people with this example of how you would in the game. If they disagree, if they are ignorant to a topic, if they simply do not mentally understand what you are speaking about or are living for, *help them understand.*

We must learn to be patient not just for our own sake, but for the sake of others. We must as a whole, find common ground to work from

This was easily the largest issue hindering the steps I allowed myself to take in life. I judged instantly and viciously, allowing no time to even comprehend why it might be somebody else was doing something so different than me. If they weren't on what my vision considered to be the right page, they were wrong and should be left in this dust. Looking back, it's easy to see now just how corrosive this state of mind can be to work, school, relationships, and our own sense of purpose & peace.

Everything is an extension of the self. Everything.

This includes other people.

To pursue a life that only accepts one side of the coin, even if it is a side rooted in knowledge & wisdom, will only keep one from reaching the ultimate state of clarity we have the potential to achieve. The Buddha didn't look at unenlightened souls with scorn or a condescending eye, but instead saw them for what they were. An extension of himself. He was a branch on a tree, just as they were. And simply because their branch currently sits in darkness, doesn't mean it won't see the light one day.

How can we ever know ourselves without attempting to understand, love and accept those who haven't had the opportunity to know themselves?

The bottom line is, we can't.

Using this state of awareness of all things being in constant motion and not judging their placement now, but understanding it as part of a process is how we can come to see the entire coin for what it is truly is. With time and effort, our own eyes will open wider than ever before. The more they open, the less we attach to wanting things to go 'our way' or for people to live 'our way of life' and instead, the more one will want to take their hands and help them wade through the turbulent stream of life.

Even for personal practices that I take part in, such as Veganism, Buddhism, etc... Is one I must constantly remind myself that I don't in fact have it fully figured out. That just because I know what I do, doesn't mean I'm any higher on the totem pole of life than those who don't take part in these practices.

Any idea of your life being is more important, or more worthy than another's simply because you are attempting to educate yourself, is a prime example of the human addiction to egotistical hierarchy. Stay humble and keep yourself way from this corrosive line of thinking.

Reading this book, practicing Buddhism, even simply eating a conscious diet *does not* place you above another soul. It simply means your soul is farther down the path than those around you. The water you wade through in your daily life may with awareness become far calmer than the rapids they trek through, but regardless we are all still trekking. We must do so together. Knowing this it simply becomes your responsibility to accept others in selfless love. Accept who they are, love them, and help them see the full spectrum of potentials awakening can bring.

It's all we can ever do.

I've noticed quite often in my life now that the more a person knows, the more bitter many of them seem to become. As if the crossing over they've experienced or the knowledge they've collected led them to despise those who don't yet know it. Often I've wondered why this is.

I think it's because when we see others not yet in touch with themselves, the planet, or the universe, we see them as remnants of our former selves. As images of the ignorance we used to harbor inside our hearts and minds. The leftovers of who 'we' were. It scares us. Imagine if you had never woken up. Imagine a life without understanding the true connection we all hold with one another and this planet. Imagine if you'd never picked up this book, or started eating healthy, or working out, or studying anything you truly love to learn about.

It's a very scary scenario. A scenario that would have resulted in you remaining in the darkness, never gaining the chance to see the bigger picture. The entire picture. But just because we now see the beauty on the front of this canvas, doesn't mean the back ceases to exist. Nor does it mean you should ignore the back because you no longer enjoy it. No. It means you must see the back, and the front for what it is and was.

A lesson.

Something that was needed to be where we are today.

On this page, in this moment, working to create the state of mind and life that can do the most for our existence.

As we come to complete and understand this step, I ask only one thing of you. From now on, be grateful for each and every moment, as well as each person you come into contact with. From your mother, to the homeless man on the side of the road, to your old best friends, and even to those who may have wronged you in the past.

Love them! Because without their place in your life, whatever it may have been, big or small, you wouldn't be here now. We are attempting to walk the line of least resistance. Of simply being. This includes acceptance of all.

The vile impacts on our lives may bring us down yes, but the amazing aspects of life bring us back up. Regardless of when and how each occur, they equal out. Leaving us where we are now. In the middle of it all. As we always have been, and always will be. Only when we come to understand the importance of the whole can we breathe deeply, peacefully, and accept each day and moment as it is. Free of bias judgement.

Full of love and light.

Chapter 11:
A New Life

Here we are. This is where our guide begins to take fruition. To transition into something real. Something tangible. Something we can manifest in each day as we work towards finding ourselves, however lost we may have been.

Imagine this guide as a game of chess. What we've learned so far; embracing fear, asking questions, loving what we do not yet know, mastering our emotions, implementing logic, accepting the totality of what we are and of what others are, these are all what we could call 'rules' to this game of life.

Easy access points to awareness.

But as I said in the beginning of Part 2, this is the path that worked best for me. Not anyone else. Why does this matter?

Because each life is far more different than they are similar. This is where you may disagree. After all you, your friends and maybe a majority of the people in your town are quite similar to each other, no? To an extent of course, they are similar. But that's only because we are looking at their image. The facade they wear each and every day. We do not see each others dreams, fears, thoughts, hobbies, and so forth. For each one of these things, our differences grow exponentially apart.

This game of life and especially the path we're trying to take isn't based on shortcuts. It's a game rooted in strategy. In understanding just where we stand on this existential chess board. And much like a chess master, if you can take these 'rules' we've come to learn, and implement them strategically in a way that benefits your life specifically, you may just win. You have the chance to become free in a way never before seen. So it makes sense that this notion, awareness only ever begins to exist when we begin to see it.

My vision for awakening in life occurred through how I had treated others prior to the major events that unfolded, as well as how I wanted to live in the days after they ended. You may have never experienced a life changing event. You may for all intensive purposes, be a good person. Regardless of whether it was due to how you were raised or if it simply occurred by natural virtue. The key is knowing that either reasoning for change is *just as valid* as any other. Mine is no more impressive than yours, and yours no more impressive than the next individual to read this book. Judgement in the form of personal hierarchy means absolutely nothing on this journey to awakening.

This is what we mean by implementing a new life. It is the process of applying these methods, these rules, in a way tailored to you and the life you live. Making awareness a strategy. Not to impress or replicate this book, or me, or what image you want these changes to create. Only by finding how these ideas best fit you, will your own path begin to form.

One does not find enlightenment by saying, "Today I will become enlightened." One finds enlightenment through self mastery. Through meditation, introspection, control, acceptance, spacial awareness and a plethora of other factors unique to the individual experience that mesh together.

Through this collaborative effort, the self grows stronger in its pursuit of peace and harmony. Until one day, it all clicks.

On it's own. Free of expectation.

When one reaches enlightenment, it's akin to waking up from a dream. We don't choose when it happens. But when it does occur, you'll know. I myself haven't reached this state, but if one day I do, so be it. What I and what you must not do however is expect it to happen. Simply being, simply strolling down this path of life with awareness is what will bring enlightenment to you. Seeking it will do nothing but prolong this.

Now there are many ways to find one's self in the chaos of our current societies. First we must warn, or better yet, inform those close to us in life of what we are attempting to pursue. Why? Because the path of least resistance wills it.

Anybody can do anything they want. That's the glory of existing in as an individual in human form. But to accomplish certain thing, transparency is the key.

When I first started to learn about Buddhism, I knew immediately it was a lifestyle I wanted to integrate into mine. So what did I do? I told my mother about the research I was doing about Buddhism, and how I found it helpful to my life. I also informed her that if she had any questions, disagreements, or worries, that I would do my best to answer them, therefore helping her understand just how pivotal these practices would be to the life I wanted to live.

After this, I told my friends. At that point in my life many people still knew me for the notorious antics I'd taken part in growing up. So when these philosophies came into my life, when I began to forge this personal path and integrate them, I figured they deserved to know why I no longer partied, why I became sober, why I ceased to speak ill of others or acted out on daily basis, so on and so forth.

Did I have to tell them? No. But when trying to live a true-to-self existence, when trying to erase the borders of you and the world as separate, informing others of the motive for such a divergence from the daily path will make the reasoning clearer. Thus leaving no room to worry about their judgement or confusion. Once they know, they know. And you are now free to continue on your path. How another may view that path or react to it is up to them.

Along these lines we have strangers we must deal with on a constant basis. When I say strangers, I want you to envision them not as random people with unknown motives, but as elegant souls who may not fully grasp what you now do, or are simply already on their own path. Much like what we talked about in Chapter 10.

The truth of the matter is most everyone on Earth is effected culturally in a more negative impact than positive. You may disagree with this, so hear me out.

We can attribute the state of the world today; War, mob mentality, materialism, and so forth to culture. Regardless of the reasoning why, it doesn't change the fact that most people on this planet simply won't understand why you do whatever it is you do. In actuality if your life is vastly different than another's, they are likely to scorn it or dislike it.

This is because human nature fears what it does not understand. Death. Sickness. Morality. Purpose. When lacking an answer, humans simply prefer to make one up, instead of accept the fact that they do not know and will not know about certain areas of existence. Ever.

As stated in Chapter 8, this awareness is one we must accept if we are ever to walk our own path. You will be judged. You will be ridiculed and you will be cast out of many current social circles. It's just the way things are these days. Don't let is discourage you however, for the truth and connection you find through universal awareness with far outweigh the temporary egotistical benefits you may currently receive from the activities or people you entertain in your life now.

On the flip side, the more you allow the outside world, with all its negative connotations attached to it to simply flow around you, the more you will notice the vivid and true souls wading strong through these murky waters. Much like you are now.

Other souls are tools. Much like our progress can be a tool to others, and this book can be a tool to you. Do not view the word in a sense of using another and discarding of them, as this is not what i mean. When I say tool, you must imagine it much like each of the steps in previous chapters. Other people are extensions of you. They are exterior vantages to not only the world, but how you describe and understand your individual 'self' in each and every moment. To truly grow, acknowledging this and allowing others to play a role in your life is key. It's not creating separation and individualizing yourself, it's simply seeing you, your family, your friends and strangers as pieces to a much larger puzzle.

To truly change and understand yourself, you must notice, accept, and attempt to understand them as well. Even if your personal biases dissuade you currently from doing so.

Analyze their judgements, their words, their actions and their justifications for why they do what they do. Simply witness them as they occur, and reflect upon that knowledge in your own personal time.

This is what it means to utilize each other's souls. It is a task many yogis and monks do on a daily basis. They see others, accept they energy they give off, and attempt to understand it for what it is at face value. Simple, effective, and a method that with time, erases actual judgement from one's mind in regards to others. It turns our life into a lesson tailored for personal growth.

We will always judge others. It is instinctual and part of the biological process that keeps us alive. The challenge is not to attach to these judgements, but to listen to them, contemplate why it may be you've had these thoughts or perceptions of said people and situations, then use that knowledge reflectively to adapt & grow from it. Good judgement is learning which perceptions to act upon, and which perceptions to grow past.

A lone figure in a hoodie walking behind you down an alley late at night is a good reason to judge the situation and assume how to go about getting keeping yourself safe.

However seeing each and every person who wears a hoodie at night as a threat is not good judgement. This subconscious typecasting process of thinking will only hurt you as you grow more accepting of it, which the majority of us do if not tailored to questioning each moment.

Just *see* what is conductive and what is not, and let go of the baggage you no longer need. Living a new life requires the exact same mental stance and strength if you are truly trying to change who you are, and grow without any unnecessary bindings.

Chapter 12
The Depths

I want you to do me a small favor. Imagine the human mind as a deep trench stretching down into the darkness of the ocean. Close your eyes for a quick moment and do this.

Now envision the water at the surface as your state of mind currently. As the way you tend to see things now. Simple, self explanatory, and most important of all, natural.

When we see the surface of an ocean or lake we say, "That is the lake. That is the ocean."

Forgetting entirely that what we're seeing is only the surface of the ocean or lake. Not the entire body of water.

In fact the surface is most likely the smallest part of this entity. Yet when you imagine your mind as this trench in the ocean, one would most likely consider the surface to be them. This couldn't be farther from the truth.

The surface of who we are, of what our Ego assumes us to be, is the easiest thing to understand about ourselves and our place here on Earth. The problem with the simplicity of this solution however is that we tend to forget to look below our own surfaces. We try to smooth the water above us, forgetting all the while that the murky water below us is what causes the ripples to begin with.

Without diving far below the surface of our own mind to confront who we truly are, a lifelong change will be impossible to implement. The lighthearted nature of what we've learned so far, (for many people) may look like it is enough to awaken unto our true selves and create a better life. But much like the fears we attribute to what we do not know, our body also reacts on a physical level, to the subconscious actions within our mind which we too fail to grasp. The biggest of these factors being doubt.

Doubt acts much like rust on a metal pipe. When you first notice this doubt, many of us either ignore it or hide it. Much the same way a construction worker may cover up a rust spot when they see it. This was the nature of what I attempted to do when I first began walking this path. I had massive layers of doubt as to why I was creating my own path and whether or not it would sustainable.

For a few years I did my best to ignore them, to pretend like they didn't exist, however this wrong action only made them grow exponentially. Growing to a point in which they overlapped my current path and began to lead me on a new, far less conductive one. Only by stepping back and confronting the depths of mms mind, doubts and all, was I able to get back on the right road so to speak.

If there is one thing you should know when approaching the road to change, it is that you *can not* trick yourself forever. Now you can try, but you will fail eventually. Why?

Because of something known in physics as Entropy.

If your unfamiliar with The Laws of Thermodynamics, which presumably you are, (don't worry though, I don't really understand them that well either) then you've probably never even heard of it. Regardless, I'll try my best to simplify Entropy as best as I can so that we can move on and not get caught up in the physics of how such a thing works.

At the most basic level you must view Entropy as chaos.

$$\text{Entropy} = \text{Law of Chaos}$$

This isn't exactly what it is, but it makes the most sense to think of it this way. What this law states is that it takes exponentially large amounts of effort to make order or sense of something. But very very little effort to make a mess of something.

If I took a bunch of neatly stacked toys, and threw them across the room, I'd have just increased the entropy of those toys.

Quite simply, I made the order of those toys far more chaotic then when they were neatly stacked. And what took me 1-2 seconds to destroy, would likely take you 5-10 minutes to fix, or to re-stack. This is because chaos is far more natural to existence as a whole than order is.

As with anything in existence, we can apply this physical law of Entropy to our mind in a conceptual format. This is what we must do in order to begin greeting doubt like family, instead of as a stranger. Think back to the trench I asked you to envision earlier. Hopefully now you can see just how easily the water below the surface can be disturbed, and because of this, realize just how important it is we calm these deep flowing movements, before we assume the surface of what we see is heathy or fully awakened in any way.

Our entire lives we've been raised on one path or another, regardless if we knew it or not. To move forward onto a new path, doubts will occur far more casually and frequently than ever before. This is simply because our mind is becoming more active, and therefore better at analyzing and critiquing new and evolving situations. Much like anything though, excessive thinking will do nothing but hurt us, and we must not fall prey to our own mind or this fundamental weakness.

For me, the more I engrossed myself in learning, the more detached I began to feel. A sort of Nihilistic mentality slowly began to sweep over me and even though I was taking in so much, a small voice in the back of my head never cease to remind me how pointless it all was.

Life, the information I was gathering, my placement here on Earth, it was all a waste if you scaled it back far enough. Even our Sun's existence, which allows life to exist at all on this massive marble, is merely a blip on a galactic radar. So why spend to much time bettering myself, why devote my life to peace, harmony and helping others if I was to die in the end? I began to convince myself it was a losing situation, my doubts began to drown me...

Then I remembered something. Something you must implement in your life and upon this path if you ever expect it to come to fruition. This realization was simple.

The purpose of life is not to win. It is to synchronize.

What I mean is that life is not a competition, it is a game! Now does it have the potential to be a competition? Of course! With yourself, your family, the society around you, and so on. You can make it as much of a competition as you want. *Or you can stop seeing personal growth as something with an endgame, (in this case Enlightenment) and start seeing it as a never ending process. From now until your last breath, the true purpose is to simply *be*.

With each day we take these practices into effect, the better we can get a just being present. Simple right?

Almost.

To step into synchronization with our new and personal paths, we must be steadfast. Not believing in the path and how it may work, but *knowing* the path will work. The difference may seems small, but if not fortified in your mind, this mental rust will spread like wildfire.

To do so there is one final step in our journey we must take. Checking our sculpture for cracks. Everything you've learned so far, all the learning you'll continue you to partake in as time goes on must be thoroughly analyzed, questioned, and picked apart so that whats left is nothing short of unbreakable in your mind. With that being said, when you finish this book, try your best to break down all the steps I've shown you so far.

View them much like a critic views a movie. Look for weakness in my wording. See if your own personal touch might make something I said better, or clearer. Don't think just because you're reading it that it must be an absolute truth, because it's not.

Even scientific journals are torn apart month after month by other scientists. Why? Because this is how progress is made.

This is how change occurs not only in the mind but in life itself. Build it up, tear it down, build it higher. So the cycle goes. This guide to awareness may be my guide currently, but I want you to make it your guide. Limiting a practice to one man's words is fine. But liberation isn't about what seems fine. It's about what we know in our heart and soul to be true.

Millions of angry individuals can rest in the grass and be at peace, but even the most peaceful man will worry when resting upon shards of glass.

So confront these doubts, not only within yourself, but within these words. Find a methodology to do this, and you will find true liberation in ways far more personal and sensible than I could ever grant you through this small bundle of words.

A (Not So) Enlightened Youth

Chapter 13
Tying the Knot
(Health & Wellness)

People never think about their shoelaces. You probably don't either. Even speaking now about shoelaces might seem an odd topic due to the trivial nature of their existence. They seem almost, unnecessary to even speak of. As if we're above them. Their purpose even speaks for itself. Shoelaces. Laces for shoes. Simple, to the point, but not inconsequential. And not to be overlooked.

Why? Because whether or not we believe it, we rely on them. Not just these laces, but a multitude of small immeasurable aspects that bind our lives together.

To truly awaken, to truly find ourselves in this never-ending fog of a system most of us live within, a system desperate to keep surrounding us, we must 'tie the knot' so to speak. One must bring all the aspects learned thus far into one entity. One well oiled machine with no signs of slowing down, and no attachment to what it once was, or what it perceives it may become. No expectations. Only progress in each moment.

We can do this simply through practice and retrospection. Not blind repetition, but repetition through the process of consistently gauging, analyzing, reworking and proceeding. We must consider using these tools and viewing the steps we've spoken on thus far as spokes on a wheel. Then we can begin to move fluently.

However there is one last step we must incorporate into our awakening, and this comes down to the physical vessel our consciousness resides within. I've read many books on spiritual growth and have become a subject in my own right to what personal development can look like and just how fast it can change. But for some reason two very important factors, (which I like to refer to as solidifiers) are almost always left out. We obsess over the mind, the way we think, and so forth. Not to say this is wrong. After all, a mental change will do far more for our understanding of existence in the long run than a physical one will. The difference is that mental change *is not everything.*

Even if this path to finding our true self takes us though 99 doors, if the last door doesn't open, we've essentially failed. This final door, this quintessential hurdle that many a skeptic and guru alike tend to forget about, is our bodily health. How we take care of our vessel, and how we energize our vessel.

The task of doing these two things in unison seems daunting and to many, a massive challenge, but in reality it isn't. The following pages will explain why.

See reading a book is simple. Taking notes is simple. Positive affirmations, meditations, mantras and so forth are simple tasks. On a physical level they require little to no effort. Nine times out of ten, when given the option to run a mile or read one chapter of a book, people will chose the book. This is understandable as well as okay, but we must learn to even out this balance beam. To inherit the endless depths of sensory information Mother Earth can bestow upon us, we must got out and embrace it.

The yogi doesn't come to know the world by spending each day in his room with nothing but books. The yogi attains these understandings by sitting under a tree, waking barefoot through the grass and treating his physical vessel like withe awareness of the fine tuned machine it has the capability to be.

Now this book is a guide, not a requirement nor a manual. The information to follow will be what has worked most efficiently for me, and has the potential to work for you as well if you allow it.

Stepping backwards to critical thinking as we spoke of earlier, I still want you to speculate over my methods. Test them. Do your own research. Find what fits you best.

Be your own Guru. Simply use my words as a starting point.

Wellness and Health will be explained in two ways from this point forward, although they are interchangeable terms. When you see Health, I want you to think diet or what you eat.

Likewise when you see Wellness, visualize it as the physical practices of finding ones self implemented via the body.

Health is fuel, wellness is exercise.

If you can master both, along with the mental steps towards awakening, you'll find it easier to get in true touch with yourself than any written visualization can give you.

Why does health matter though? This might seem like an honest inconsequential thing to ask and/or ignore, but doing so will only create a rift within. Health is paramount to our spiritual and physical self because it is the fuel by which we thrive. Without this fuel, we would die. It's really as simple as that.

Granted we now live in an era where what we see and call 'food' comes in millions of odd, tasty combinations in a range of sizes and flavors. But this is for the most part, is the largest illusion mankind currently knows.

Processed sugars, cancer causing preservatives and chemical cocktails are used to make what we put in our body seem edible . Yet these 'foods' are one of, if not the direct root to the heath epidemic that currently plagues most first world nations. If you're anything like me, you were raised in a family that didn't know any better. So if this is your first time reading anything like this, do not take the information that follows and use it to harbor anger towards those who've wronged you. They simply didn't know any better either. What we eat will either kill us or strengthen us far beyond the current physical state of most people around the world. It's a simple choice, no more, no less.

What do I mean by all this? Just one thing.

If what you are eating is not comprised of fruits, vegetables, grains or greens, (along with B12) you shouldn't be eating it.

Period.

Now, this is what is called conventionally a 'Vegan' diet, but that term currently tends to carry connotations with it that takes away from what the diet really is; The healthiest diet a human can physically eat. This is not an opinion, it is a *fact*.

Cognitive dissonance and cultural normalities have conditioned us to despise this fact. We grow up with a constant stream of nostalgia pertaining to food. When going out to eat, munching on steak or burgers and even ice cream, is not only nostalgic for us but tasty.

So you may ask yourself,

"Do I really need to give all that up to make true progress?"

No. Of course you don't. You can meditate daily, practice yoga and mindfulness, all while going home to a steak dinner every night. It is doable yes, but it will only take you so far.

I've spoken of this before and will do so again now, only by fully cutting animal cruelty out of what you eat, can true unaltered peace of mind be achieved.

There is no way around this fact.

This is due in part to the Pillar of Right Action. A core pillar of the Eightfold Path and the best place to start when analyzing your diet. Right Action simply means to be fully aware of the actions you take in daily life. Because of this, to live harmoniously with the planet, our actions must cause the least amount of harm we physically can dish out in regard to the actions we take. From driving a Prius versus a Diesel, to eating a meal that does not promote the suffering of other innocent species on this planet.

Bottom line; To eat meat or any animal byproduct, is to promote oppression over another species instead of living side by side with it. Regardless if you intend to do so or not.

Any action or diet you have taken part in up until today does not matter. You now know the truth. The responsibly to change is now in your hands. From this page forward, the diet you chose, is a reflection of the light not only within yourself, but the light you are emanating onto others. Human and inhuman.

This is not a political stance. It is an ethical stance. And to find ones' self, we must return to our roots and suppress this oppressive diet we have been so engrained with.

If you're still torn over what I'm saying, I only ask that you research the benefits of a Vegan diet in depth, both for your body and for the planet. The facts will speak for themselves.

I cannot speak for every person who comes into an awakening in their life, but I will say this; Since cutting animals out of my diet, my personal connection to the Earth and to myself has grown tenfold. I physically feel more intertwined with other species and with this ecosystem because I know subconsciously that what I eat is in an attempt to help the planet, not hurt it. This selflessness will show itself in each meal you participate in. It is one of the key instances where you don't revert back to mindfulness, but mindfulness comes to you.

Moving on from one's diet, we have the final pillar of our path to set in stone. The last piece of the puzzle.

Physical Wellness.

This wellness, (much like our diet) is not mandatory. It only exists to tie this knot tighter than it's current state.

This is because our body is the physical manifestation of connection to the universe. Consciousness allows us to perceive, our bodies allow us to physically experience. A picture of a waterfall is beautiful, yet pales in comparison to actually witnessing the power and beauty of one in real life.

Expanding upon this, if the body is not tuned to experience the world on a tangible level, it only creates limitations. A body in shape will always absorb vibrational energy and sensory information in all forms. Much more efficiently than a body struggling to function. It's akin to covering one eye. Yes, you can see. But your field of vision and depth perception will be skewed against your favor.

Finding a method of wellness however that fits our lives is up for debate, and can become a double edged sword in the same light.

The purpose of staying in shape is to allow our body to thrive as efficiently as possible, yet many people let the results they may receive from proper diets and physical workouts shift their personal view into a more egotistical light. If you are to focus intently on wellness, it should not be to gloat at the results you see in the mirror, or to compare yourself to others practicing the same methods. This misguided attention will only create an internal rift mentally. The objective isn't creating something for others to see, the objective is creating something that connects us on a deeper level to our physical nature.

So how do we go about this?

Physical progress can be reached in many ways. I personally find two major methods not only highly spiritual, but the most effective in their impacts upon the entire body.

The first and most important one focuses on our core. The heart, lungs and other vital organs; Cardio.

Health isn't measured in how large your biceps are, health is measured by how well our organs can function when pushed to their limits. Cardio implements itself not only due to the way it strengthens our core, but with how it keeps us present, in the moment, and tranquil. This is achieved through forced mindfulness due to awareness of breath.

When practicing cardio, one cannot help but regulate and focus on the breaths they take. This by default through regular practice, places you in what's known as the 'zone'. A state of mental and physical flow many athletes find themselves in during clutch moments. A state of thoughtlessness, serenity, and immediate understanding of the exact moment.

The greatest methods of cardio, (in my personal view) come in the form of running, swimming, and biking. Whichever outlet you have the greatest amount of access to is preferable to start with, but as with anything, attempt all methods if possible and decide on which ones work best for you. Research is key and many different factors go into these methods. Each brings with it its own cardio and full body benefits. Running may being the easiest, but Biking and Swimming enact a more complete bodily workout.

Harnessing cardio allows the interior aspects of the body to flourish, but aside from this there is another   bodily art form that gives each person the opportunity to master their physical body through motion, flow and flexibility.

Yoga.

Stemming from Pre-Vedic India, (current estimates begin roughly 5,000 years ago with the oldest reaching 10,000 years) this almost flawless art form in relation to the human body is essential to our awakening, as the practice of Yoga not only impacts our physical body, but spiritual self and universal connection held within as well.

This occurs due to the root nature of Yogic practice; Physical discipline. It allows us to push our body to its limits not only in dexterity, but creatively as well. From this we can come to know our body entirely. Greater still is the low learning curve that Yoga holds, allowing beginners much like many of you, to implement it into your unique lifestyle as quickly or slowly as you'd like. There is no requirement to Yogic practice, only dedication and positive intent in the moment and in the movements of the body.

Due in part to the ancient history of Yoga, there are hundreds of different branches ranging from intense full body workouts, to mantra-based, slow moving flow sessions.

As I've stated before, I only ask you to take my words into consideration, and following this, to attempt any other methods you may find interest in from which you can place into your life.

After much trial and error, I found the school of Haṭhavidyā, (otherwise known as Hatha Yoga) to be the perfect balance when factoring in both mental and physical consistency. Why? Because as stated earlier, placing ones self in the 'zone' allows us to be one with the moment in its entirety. Hatha Yoga, (being an almost purely physical branch of Yoga) allows us this opportunity to simply be with the moment, with our body, and with the postures we are practicing.

Certain branches of Yoga may contain chants or other vocal tools yes. To me though, this takes away from the body and unintentionally ads a level of self judgment or focus on what we say, how we pronounce it and so on. This ultimately takes away from allowing the body to be at peace. Simply put, if it isn't necessary, you don't need to implement it.

Much like the Eightfold Path which exists as a core pillar of Buddhism, Yoga too has a similar pillar, known as The Eight Legs of Yoga. The physical leg, (known in Sanskrit as The Asanas) is a totality of the bodily movements or poses one takes part in during Yoga. Even sitting in a Half-Lotus during meditation is one form of these Asanas.

This physical focus on the Asanas is the key pillar of Hatha Yoga in it's most current westernized form. Partially explaining why this method is the most common form of Yoga undertaken in the western world.

Through consistent Hatha practice, one is allowed the ability to increase strength, but more importantly, flexibility and familiarity with the body and it's positionings. This becomes majorly prevalent when practicing sitting for meditation, and is why Hatha is considered such a key factor in the individual search for Enlightenment.

The depths of Yoga, regardless of branch, are an extension of our awakening. If we can engrain such a practice into our lives, it ceases to be tasks and begins to be something much more natural. Like eating. or sleeping. With this we can grow, move, and flow both mentally and physically in ways never before experienced. Much like the mind, our physical body with the right fuel and movement may finally achieve a state of absolute relaxation.

Only through this relaxation can we detach from the person we define ourselves as now, and move on to greater planes of growth & development.

Chapter 14
Reflections
(A Message for the Future)

We've finally arrived at our destination, however temporary it may turn out to be. Up until this point I've been speaking to you from what may seem like a higher vantage. A place farther along the path in essence, but much like any path, we can only travel so far so quickly.

I speak to you now as I have attempted to throughout this guide; As a friend. Someone standing by your side.

Finding one's self may seem to be no easy task, but the more we learn and implement the practices covered in the last few chapters, the easier it becomes. Not just for you, but for me as well. After all I'm still young too.

Some of you reading this will be younger than me, some older. This alone shows how little it matters when it comes to where we perceive to be along this path. We're all just on it.

No hierarchy. Just progressing.

With that being said we must now step past the pages of this book. Remember these words, use them, but don't allow yourself to get stuck on them and only them. I use this path almost subconsciously now in my daily life, but as with any method of progress, I am always on the lookout for ways to better implement it, improve it, and expand upon it. Maybe one day you'll find yourself awake in such a state you must supersede my guide and write your own. In fact this is an outcome I for one would truly love to see.

The title of this chapter is called 'Reflections' not to reflect upon what we've learned so far though. After all, if one needs a full chapter to reflect upon concepts spoken about in the chapters before, the story may seem a little too weak for advocating it as a full fledged lifestyle. The name of this chapter is called what it is because it encapsulates what we must be when we put down this book, and walk out into our lives;

Reflections.

We are not the sole aspect of any image. Though our eyes and ego may assume this to be true, it is only part of an eternal illusion. As the honorable Ram Dass would say, we must see ourselves as a reflection of the whole. And through this use what we've learned here, to live as such. Reflecting the true nature of reality upon the world.

This reality is love. Unconditional and free of expectation.

This guide means nothing if we cannot express the truths it brings us to others. Awakening too means nothing if we cannot return as servants of this truth. From Gurus to Bodhisattvas and so forth, we must help others make progress along their own paths. This is our karmic purpose. This is speaking as the whole, not as a mere part of it. Understanding and expressing what we have learned so far and what we will come to learn as life flows onward is the key to being a true reflection.

This book is only a small piece of the reflections I am attempting to show you and others. With time more will come. But as always, one step at a time.

With wisdom comes the newfound responsibility to pay it forward. This could be to the world, or to a close friend, or to a complete stranger. After all, this is now your path.

I wish you luck upon it, and I'll see you down the road.

- Koi Fresco

Made in the USA
Middletown, DE
23 August 2019